MY AMERICAN LIFE

CONGRESSWOMAN
LAUREN BOEBERT

BOMBARDIER
BOOKS

Published by Bombardier Books
An Imprint of Post Hill Press
ISBN: 978-1-63758-204-6
ISBN (eBook): 978-1-63758-205-3

My American Life
© 2022 by Congresswoman Lauren Boebert
All Rights Reserved

Post Hill Press
New York • Nashville
posthillpress.com

Published in the United States of America
1 2 3 4 5 6 7 8 9 10

This book is dedicated to my four boys, who I promised would never grow up in a socialist country, and to every American who supports me standing up for their God-given rights and belief in freedom.

CONTENTS

A GUN-THEMED RESTAURANT OWNER
BECOMES A GUN RIGHTS ADVOCATE

TO RUN OR NOT TO RUN? THAT IS THE QUESTION

ONE UPSET DOWN, ONE MORE TO GO

MRS. BOEBERT GOES TO WASHINGTON

JUST THE BEGINNING

FOREWORD

Lauren Boebert's love of country, her commitment to conservatism, and her enthusiasm to help get our country back on track made it easy for me to endorse her candidacy for Congress.

Lauren Boebert is not only my colleague in Congress, but also a friend whom the American people can count on to be a fearless fighter for liberty.

For those of you who have never met Lauren, she is a true patriot. When Lauren says she is serving to make sure her four boys never grow up in a socialist nation, she means it with all her heart. Family means the world to her, and her four boys are the driving force that motivates her to work so hard for our shared conservative values.

Her authenticity is rare, and it's no surprise that she is not a typical member of Congress. In fact, Lauren had never even run for public office before she won her seat, because she was running her own business and raising her family.

Lauren speaks from her heart about her relationship with God, her motivation to serve, and her experiences during her first year in Congress. It is clear to me that Lauren cares deeply about the people she represents, and they love her passion to fight.

Her story is one that so many Americans who've worked hard to overcome challenges and yet risen to the occasion can identify with. And for that very reason – because she rejected the liberal trap of dependency and worked hard to achieve the American dream – she is relentlessly vilified by the Left.

As you read , I think you will appreciate learning about the influences of Lauren's upbringing and her experiences that led her to Congress.

Our nation needs more Representatives like Lauren who are committed to the fight to save our country, who work tirelessly to enact conservative policies, and who aren't afraid of the Left-wing mob.

United States Senator Ted Cruz

INTRODUCTION

"**Y**ou are eager. You are excited. You are what we need in America. Don't ever let anyone tell you that you don't have a role in this country, in our future!"

It's true! And it's just as true today as it was when I spoke those words before a group of eager, free-thinking, and patriotic young women at the 2020 Turning Point USA Student Action Summit. In that group of doe-eyed, enthusiastic young women, I saw the future—although someone rightfully opened my eyes to the fact that they are not the *future* but rather the "now." I couldn't agree more.

Now is the time to fight for freedom of thought.

Now is the time to stand up for diversity of ideas.

Now is the time to say "no more" to the evil that seeks to destroy our nation.

Now is the time to embolden my generation—the oft-maligned millennial generation—to stand for conservative values.

Now is the time to persevere and pursue dreams.

And if you don't believe opportunity and the American Dream are yours for the taking, look no further than me—a thirtysomething mother of four from a small rural town who has a GED, no college degree, and no formal training. I grew up poor, raised by a practically single mother on welfare. Yet here I am, a successful business owner proudly serving Colorado's 3rd Congressional District as a United States representative.

From rural Colorado to Capitol Hill. Only in America.

If there were such a job title as "Spokeswoman for American Opportunity," I could easily fill it. By God's grace, I am the personification of the American Dream, and here's the special sauce—you can be too! With a work ethic, tenacity, and a love of country, you can achieve anything in America. Contrary to what an Establishment liberal will tell you, you CAN be whatever you want to be in this great country of ours. I'm proof.

Success in America is a choice. The choice young Americans make today will determine not just their future but the country's future too. There are two sides to my generation: There are the smart, hard workers who give it their all, knowing success depends on them—the ones who choose to take ownership of their future, pull up their bootstraps, and make it happen! Then there are the lazy, entitled ne'er-do-wells who believe government and the successful owe them something—the ones who choose to sit idly by, not make an effort to live up to their potential, and then blame the "haves" when they "have not." If I'd stood around with my hand out when I had nothing, where would I be today? Certainly not in Congress.

I wasn't raised in a fancy home with a fancy education. I worked at a McDonald's. I proudly represented the Golden Arches and learned valuable lessons about hard work and an honest day's pay for an honest day's work. It helped shape who I am today.

But the measurement of success goes so far beyond money, material possessions, or position. Ask yourself, "What difference am I making in my community?" "What impact do I have on others?" "Am I a catalyst for change?" After all, there will always be a changing of the guard. Someone will have to answer the call. Will it be you?

I went to DC to make sure my boys don't grow up to live in a socialist nation, which is where we're headed if people who have common sense don't speak up. But before I even thought about running for Congress, I got involved at the grassroots level in my community, where real change can be made. I stood up to local government officials when their pandemic "powers" overreach nearly ruined my business and the livelihood of all my employees. I showed up at a rally for failed Presidential candidate Robert Francis "Beto" O'Rourke and challenged him to explain why he wanted to trample over the Second Amendment of the Constitution of the United States on his way to confiscating your guns. I wasn't a politician. I was a small business owner, a mother, wife, a concerned citizen, and I was ticked off. So there I was, going toe-to-toe with a man—the embodiment of entitlement—who fancied himself "called" to be President, or as he famously told *Vanity Fair*, "I'm just born to be in it." It's amazing what a concerned citizen can do when they remember the government is here to serve the people—the people are not here to serve the government.

Influence doesn't necessarily come easy, but it also doesn't come with any prerequisites. It doesn't require a degree from a hoity-toity college, a privileged background, a huge Instagram following, powerful connections, or a big bank account. As I'll say repeatedly, with a work ethic, tenacity, and a love of God, family, and country, you can, and will, make a difference!

There are so many people who work to keep the government accountable—and who've helped to make America the greatest country in the whole of humankind. Our country stands on the self-evident truths that all men (and women) are created equal, that we're endowed by our Creator with certain unalienable rights, that among these are life, liberty, and the pursuit of happiness. Countless stories bear witness to principled people fighting for the American way of life.

I'm one of them.

★ ★ ★

A TOUGH START

★ ★ ★

CHAPTER 1

From Florida to Colorado to Florida to Colorado

The first campaign advertisement I launched after I won my Republican primary was called "Breaking the Cycle of Poverty." The ad highlighted how I had overcome the challenges of growing up poor. The cycle of poverty is a very real thing, and far too many people in our country don't know any other way of life. I lived it, and I can tell you it's a tough cycle to break, no matter how hard you try, because it turns out hope and change is easier said than done. A lack of job skills, instability at home, family members addicted to drugs and alcohol, and a dependency on the government all reduce the odds of someone breaking that cycle of poverty. I'm sure there are also powerful statistics that show how being a single mother makes it that much harder.

Welcome to my childhood.

I was born in Altamonte Springs, Florida, a bustling suburb in the northern part of Orlando. Growing up, I didn't know my biological father. He pressured Mom to get an abortion, but thank God, she refused. My mom is my best friend, so it's important you know that when I talked to her about this book, she encouraged me to tell you just the way things were, so here it goes.

Mom was an eighteen-year-old high school dropout struggling to make ends meet. She attended beauty school for a while, then cut hair to put money in her pocket. The struggle was real. Since Mom was still a teenager when she had me, besides being a parent, she wanted to be my friend too. Mom was not authoritarian. She wasn't all too interested in being a disciplinarian, and she has always been my best friend. I consider myself lucky for that. She'd also be the first to tell anyone she wasn't a typical mom, but her parents were, and that made me lucky too.

My grandparents filled what I considered to be the traditional mother and father roles in my young life. They helped with my foundational beliefs. They're the ones who taught me to be responsible, respectful to elders, and to attend church. Granny and Papa wanted me to grow up knowing what it meant to be a good person. We lived with them for the first four years of my life. Then Mom decided she'd venture out on her own. But at first, it wasn't what one might call "easy."

We didn't have a particularly stable home life, and Mom's choices in men weren't, well, let's say they weren't exactly the best. When I was four, Mom, who was then twenty-two, met a guy I will call "Mike" for the purposes of this book. He was visiting from Colorado and staying with one of her friends. The second the friend introduced the two of them, sparks flew. Their connection was so strong that Mike immediately made the pitch for Mom to visit him when he got back to Colorado. For him, the timing couldn't have been any better. But for Mom, in hindsight, it could not have been worse. She accepted his offer mainly to spite my grandmother, who was adamantly against her making such a foolish move at such a young age.

Up to this point, Mom had been in an on-again, off-again relationship with a successful Florida business owner named Jimmy. It was during one of those off-again times when she met Mike. Mom figured she and Jimmy weren't a thing anymore so she could date whomever she pleased. Besides, Colorado and the Rocky Mountains sounded like a great escape for a wayward twenty-two-year-old. Nevertheless, she had reservations. Mom didn't know Mike all that well and was nervous about traveling so far on her own. Besides, she couldn't just leave her four-year-old daughter alone for a week. What should she do? Mom's solution, and a questionable one at that, was to bring her pregnant friend along with us on a Greyhound bus from Florida to Colorado. Why either one of them thought this was a good idea, we'll never know, but it happened.

So, a toddler, her mom, and a pregnant woman get on a bus.... It sounds like the opening line to a good joke, but there was nothing funny about this trip. Being pregnant and riding cross-country on a bus made my mom's friend sick—so sick, in fact, that she needed all of us to get off the bus and wait for the next bus while she recovered. On the next bus, she got sick again, and we had to get off that one too. This was clearly going to be a very long trip, but Mom was determined to get to Colorado and see Mike, so she decided to leave her friend and me at the station and hop on the next bus by herself. Great. I got to ride across the country with a cranky, sick, pregnant lady I barely knew.

Mom made it to Colorado and enjoyed two days alone with Mike before I, along with her road-weary friend, rolled into town. Mike lived in Aurora with two dogs in a small, cramped apartment. So here we were, three adults, one toddler, and two dogs packed into one apartment—not exactly the brochure picture for life in the Rocky Mountains. But, hey, I liked the dogs, and Mom liked Mike. They had a great time together. Clearly. Mike was now asking my mom to leave Florida and move in with him in Colorado.

This guy moved fast but Mom, well, she moved faster. She turned Mike down and instead got back together with Jimmy in Florida and moved us in with him at his beach house. Suddenly life was good. It felt like I had a family. The three of us together, eating and laughing at our dinner table and going for long walks on the beach where we collected seashells, felt like living in a fairy tale. Jimmy was kind, and I was sure he was going to be the dad I never had. I liked the idea of that a lot because of the connection we were making. He and I had already spoken with a secret code word, "Slatterslaw," that I am quite confident meant, "I love you." It meant a lot to me.

Unfortunately, he never had a chance to be that guy. Just as quickly as we moved in, we moved out. Mom suddenly decided to dump Jimmy and move us in with Mike in Colorado.

In case you haven't figured it out by now, my mother could be, in a word, "flighty." Perhaps that is where my need for adventure originates from.

My head was spinning. Why wouldn't it be? I was a little kid who didn't understand why things were changing so quickly. Oh well, good-bye beach house, hello Aurora, Colorado apartment. I hoped this would be a fun adventure.

It wasn't.

In no time at all, it was clear that Mom had made a terrible, terrible mistake. Life with Mike was miserable. First, as if it wasn't already overcrowded with the three of us and the two dogs in a little apartment, on most weekends, Mike's son, who was two years older than me, would come to stay with us too. Ironically, that was the one positive to this whole arrangement. He and I had an instant brother-sister relationship, where we'd often play and, just as often, fight together. Generally, though, we found a way to get along. Truth be told, having another kid around was fun for me.

Second, Mike was abusive toward my mother. We'd barely unpacked the boxes before it began. He'd yell at her, push her, and slap her around. I'd get so mad that I'd stomp my little feet and throw things at him to get him to stop. He wouldn't. I repeatedly called my grandparents for help, telling them how bad things were and how Mike would hit my mom. They begged Mom to come home. Mike would then beg her to stay, promising he would behave better—a typical pattern of domestic abusers. The process would repeat itself often over the years.

Mom didn't go home to Florida. Instead, she stayed, and before long, she was pregnant with my first baby brother, Benjamine, who I still call "Benny." By the time Benny was born, Mike's behavior had worsened. He drank heavily, stayed out late, and often missed work.

When Mike's behavior got out of hand, Mom would threaten to move back to Florida. But then, Mike would take Benny and disappear for hours, sometimes days. Mom was too terrified to move, fearing what Mike might do to her, me, or Benny.

An already horrible situation kept getting worse.

We were stuck.

Years later, Mom told me she was ashamed she'd made such a bad decision to stay with Mike. She admitted she was afraid of him and that her concern for both my and my brother's safety kept her from leaving. She felt trapped. Mom wanted her kids to have a dad, even if he was a bad dad. In hindsight, that sounds crazy. But at the time, her fear of the unknown outweighed the tragedy of the known.

Instead of moving away, Mom got pregnant again with her second and third sons. Not long after that, we found ourselves in Montbello, one of the poorest neighborhoods in Denver. We also found ourselves on food stamps.

I remember going to the grocery store and paying for food with an EBT card. I remember using "Monopoly" money to buy food. I remember going to the food bank, a large warehouse where we'd stand in line to pick up containers of food alongside lots of people who looked like they were struggling to get by. Was that us? Were we so poor we couldn't afford to buy food?

Mike was rarely working now. Mom was busy taking care of her new babies at home, and I was spending most of my time there with my brothers, offering to play "mom" by changing their diapers, feeding them, and generally looking out for them. I loved my brothers, and I loved being their big sister. To this day, they see me as more of a motherly figure than a sister.

Mom would talk about finding work in a salon but was warned she'd lose her welfare checks if she did that. They said it would cost her more to do that than to just stay at home. It was official—Mom and our family had become dependent on the government for our survival.

I never forgot this.

CHAPTER 2

Teen Angst & the Art of the Fight

The one positive during this time was school. I really liked it, probably because Mike wasn't there. I liked the structure and studied hard to get good grades and earn praise from my teachers. I was fitting in with the other kids, listening to rap music, and dancing with my friends after school. I was good enough at freestyle rap battles that I had earned their respect.

As I got older, I was also learning to defend myself and distrust authority. It may have been a lesson I learned from Mike, or it may have been something I learned while I was at school. There, disagreements were often settled by schoolyard fights, not by tattling to the principal. I was no angel myself. I got into a few fights when I felt mistreated and thought I had to stick up for myself. I got beat up, and I fought back, but I didn't tell any adults about it.

One year, I'd been assigned an English teacher who clearly had given up on teaching by the time I took her class. She seemed bitter about the misdeeds of students from years past and took it out on us. Her go-to punishment was to have the entire class write repetitive statements about our collective poor behavior. It was almost like the opening of *The Simpsons*, where Bart is writing repetitive sentences on the chalkboard. I hated being punished for something I didn't do. I dreaded this class because it felt like a waste of time, and I wasn't good at hiding it. Tensions escalated, and my mom had to get involved, which resulted in me being switched to another English class.

This new class didn't get off to the best of starts, though. A student aide overheard my former English teacher talking to my new teacher and making fun of my mother and me. She put down my mom's clothes and said other horrible things about Mom. As I'd soon see, her words either rubbed off on my new teacher, or this new teacher was just as bad as the old one. One day, she falsely accused the entire class of poking fun at a special-ed classmate who was absent that day. The teacher said we shouldn't speak ill toward anyone who wasn't present to defend themselves. Obviously, she didn't apply that idea to my old teacher who'd been putting down Mom and me. As for the special-ed student—we hadn't been making fun of him. The opposite was true. We were saying nice things. Everyone in class liked him and went out of their way to look out for him. It offended me that my teacher, someone who I should respect, was falsely accusing everyone of something I knew not to be true.

Just then, the lightbulb went off over my head that she was guilty of doing what she accused us of doing. I decided to call her on it. I asked the teacher, in front of the entire class, why she had spoken ill about my mother and me behind our backs. She immediately became defensive and realized she'd been caught in her own hypocrisy. The class had a good laugh. I felt vindicated by standing up for my mom and me and, indirectly, for our friend who wasn't there that day.

If you've seen me speak at a campaign event, a rally, a news conference, or to Beto O'Rourke, then you know I've got a fire in my belly for justice. Maybe the spark was lit that day.

Back at home, by the time I was a teenager, Mike finally found some self-awareness. It looked like even he was tired of his act. One of his buddies who'd found work in Aspen was encouraging him to take a job there along with him. My mom encouraged Mike to take it, and he did.

So, we were on the move. Again. We left Montbello and headed three hours west to Rifle, which was about an hour and a half away from Aspen. I was glad to move. Rifle was fresh and new. We were living in a nicer place—a benefit of gainful employment. Mike was earning money, and we weren't going to the food bank. There were small steps taking place in our life that made me feel like we were getting on a better track.

I liked my new school and teachers, and I was eager to get involved in cheerleading. I was also getting a taste of the independence that comes from growing up, and I loved it.

CHAPTER 3

Living on the Government's Dime Is No Way to Live

There are a million ways my childhood experiences can be dissected and analyzed. There are plenty of Democrats that would argue my circumstances begged for their welfare programs and that without them, our family's struggles would have been far worse. I don't believe that. I think their programs enabled Mike and my mom to avoid tough decisions and encouraged poor decision-making.

Mike and my mom were capable of work, but the system encouraged them to game the system. If they weren't married, Mom was eligible for welfare. If she had more kids, she got more welfare. If she didn't work, she got even more welfare. What a system.

The "head" of our household was unstable and seemed unemployable. Mike bounced from job to job and often went into violent, alcohol-fueled rages. He crossed the line so often that Mom would kick him out of the house.

In 2012, our lives got a lot better. Mom went out and earned money on her own and finally started getting back on track. There's plenty of work to do to help more people get back on track. We owe it to our country to make the system better.

While we should always supply a safety net for those most in need, that net needs to be a helping hand up, not a handout for those who can otherwise find a way forward. Too many people capable of work are relying on the labor of others to support them. Democrats will send you money. Democrats will pay for your food. Democrats will pay for your health care. All you must do is vote for them, and they'll do it all for you! So, Mom always voted for Democrats. She believed their promises and fell prey to their argument for dependency on the government. No one who votes that way ever seems to realize that the price we all pay for that dependency is much higher than anyone can calculate. It also strips people of their dignity.

Mom was dependent on Mike. Mom was dependent on the government. It didn't matter how poorly she was treated. She needed both to survive, but neither made life any better nor did they propel her forward. Mom was essentially treading water. It wasn't until she decided to become independent that she finally started to pull away from both.

It's been a driving motivation in my life to make sure I never go back to that way of life. I've always worked hard to make sure it doesn't happen. Now, I want to be a role model for those who want to make it on their own and feel the same sense of pride and dignity that comes with earning your own paycheck.

Life for me has had plenty of challenges, some I inflicted on myself and others that just came my way. But I honestly believe that living free and depending on yourself and on God is how you pursue happiness.

I learned this lesson early on—while still in high school. Though I was busy with classes and cheerleading, which I just loved, I wanted to earn my own money. Life on welfare sucked.

So, did somebody say McDonald's?

★ ★ ★ CHAPTER 4 ★ ★ ★

McQuitting High School

My high school friends were great—and the best ones were the ones with cars because they gave me rides to eat lunch off campus. What high school kid doesn't like getting food from somewhere other than the cafeteria? But the downside to eating off campus was I needed a buck or two to buy some lunch at McDonald's. The Hot 'n Spicy McChicken was my absolute favorite lunch, and I did everything I could to make sure I ate at McDonald's every single school day.

I had to get scrappy to make that a reality. I didn't have a job, and Mom wasn't about to give me the money, so I'd keep an eagle eye out for loose change at school and in the parking lot. But that was about to change (pun intended). One day, I recognized a classmate working behind the McDonald's counter and thought how nice it would be to stop scavenging for nickels and dimes. So I had a thought—what if I got a job there? Then I could eat as many chicken sandwiches as I wanted. I talked to the classmate, who told me employees got food at half-price if they ate it at the restaurant, and it was free if you worked regular shifts. Free?! Wow! I brought home a job application.

Despite the exciting thought of getting free or half-priced McDonald's, the application sat on my dresser for a few days. I was too nervous to fill it out because I'd never worked before. I was only fifteen. But the more I thought about it, the more I wanted to be able to buy things all on my own. I asked Mom what she thought. She was always pressing me for good grades, always saying how important my high school education was for my future, but she didn't say, "No." She told me if I took a job to be sure it didn't interfere with school. Awesome! I got good grades, so no problem there. I didn't think it mattered anyway. I didn't see things the way Mom did because, hey, I was a stubborn teenager.

I turned in the application, and a manager asked me to come back the next day for an interview. This was all so new, and I wanted to make sure I was prepared. I showed up to the McDonald's an hour early and waited in the dining room. I didn't know what to expect. I figured they'd quiz me, and of course, I'd ace it. I mean, I loved eating at McDonald's. If they asked me what was in a Big Mac, gosh darn it, I was going to nail it—two all-beef patties, special sauce, lettuce, cheese, pickles, onions on a sesame seed bun. I could hear the jingle in my head. And now, I'm sure you do too.

The interview came and went without a pop quiz or a jingle, and I got a job offer. The manager told me that because I was only fifteen, I couldn't work more than a few hours during the week and some on the weekend. I told her I'd work every hour she'd let me.

I couldn't wait to start. I had a job to do and Hot 'n Spicy McChicken sandwiches to eat!

When I charged through my front door carrying a hand-me-down green McDonald's work shirt, black polyester pants, and visor, I was on cloud nine. I washed and ironed them, put them on, and modeled them in front of the mirror all night. I spent hours pretending to say "Hello" to my customers at my register in my restaurant. "Hello, sir. Would you like fries with that? That'll be a dollar six, please. Here's your change. Have a great day!" I was McLovin' it before that was even a thing.

Failure was not an option. I was bound and determined to succeed at my new job. Not even the polyester pants deterred me, which, since I was a high school cheerleader, might have surprised a few of my classmates. I promised Mom that my schedule wouldn't get in the way of school and told her not to worry. Yes, she still worried about me.

Every weekday, I had cheerleading practice from four to five in the afternoon and games on Friday nights. So, the plan was for me to work from six to eight on weekday nights and six-hour shifts on Saturdays and Sundays. By my math, I was quickly going to be rich.

My heart was racing when I arrived for my first day on the job. It was all so new and exciting, plus I felt so grown-up. The manager assigned me to work the front register and cautioned that I wasn't to leave it and that I'd be timed for performance. Also, that a smile was a part of my uniform, and my uniform had to be always worn properly. McDonald's was all business.

Those few hours came and went in a flash. After I clocked out, I went home with a real sense of accomplishment. Not only did I love it, but I was also good at it. But earning a paycheck wasn't the only thing I wanted. I also wanted to be a standout employee—the best front register worker the Rifle McDonald's had ever known. So, right there at home, I started practicing. I got out a pen and paper and drew a picture of the front of the register, every button with every name of every item—Big Mac, Quarter Pounder, medium fries, and so on. I memorized every key. Nothing would slow me down. I was fast, I was proud, and I was happy.

Even at that age, I believed that a good worker, one who'd be successful, had to go beyond what was being asked of them. But in my zeal to learn more about the restaurant, I'd sometimes leave the register when there weren't any customers so I could help in other areas. That was a no-no, and I'd be gently reprimanded. I guess I figured that if I saw how other tasks were being done, I'd already know how to do them if I got assigned those tasks.

My goal was to be promoted from the dining room register to the drive-thru register. The ones who worked there were the fastest, best employees on the team. They were under constant pressure because they were on a timer every minute they spent at the drive-thru window. You might not realize it when you run to grab a burger, but there's some impressive workflow at that window. Those workers are pressed to move traffic through quickly while providing service with a smile. I studied them from the front register and was already thinking about how to prep the bags to deliver the food more quickly. The real hook for me was the chance to wear the cool-as-all-get-out headset and to hear my voice on the speaker. After just a few weeks behind the front counter, I got my shot! It was even cooler than I thought it would be.

If you ever want to learn how to stay focused and be kept accountable by your boss and your customers, work one day at a McDonald's drive-thru and see what happens when you accidentally put a small fry in the bag instead of a large one!

After a couple of weeks, the day I'd been waiting for finally arrived. Payday. In my hands, I held my first-ever paycheck. This wasn't an electronic deposit; it was an actual check, and it was mine. I had earned it and was so over-the-moon proud of it. Then, like so many other young people before me, I learned about Uncle Sam. I opened the envelope, but where was all my money?! Who was FICA, and why were they taking so much of my money? Interestingly, it's a question I still ask today.

When I got home, Mom was waiting for me at the top of the stairs. I handed her my check, and we hugged. She was so proud. This was a momentous occasion, and we needed to celebrate. As I recall, I had a little over one hundred dollars. We decided to splurge for a spaghetti dinner, which was a huge deal for us. Usually, dinner at home was some version of Hamburger Helper. Not that night!

Over dinner, Mom and I talked about what to do with all my newly earned cash. It came down to gas money and socks, and I didn't even have to choose between the two. I could afford both now. We decided I should give my friends forty dollars to help with the gas for all the rides they gave me and that I should treat myself to brand-new socks. This might not sound like much, but we'd been so poor that I'd been sharing socks with my little brothers. I went out and bought little white ankle socks with "Hanes" stitched in pink letters—guaranteeing the boys would never want to wear them. I sure was happy to finally have socks to call my own.

As a girl, I also had other needs the boys would never understand.

Sometimes kids grow up thinking crazy things—like if you break your arm, it actually falls off. For me, for some inexplicable reason, I thought tampons were extremely expensive and something I couldn't afford. Who could buy them if they were fifty dollars or more? When I was old enough to need them, I still had that question. But I was too embarrassed to learn what tampons actually cost because there was no way I could afford them. When I couldn't find any tampons in our house, I didn't want to burden Mom by asking for money to buy them. This was long before my McDonald's income started pouring in, and this problem needed to be solved right away.

I'd heard on the radio that students in my area could turn in their report cards and the local bank would give them ten dollars for every A and five dollars for every B. I had all A's, so that meant I could get sixty dollars! Easy money, problem solved. I walked down to the bank, and I handed in my report card. But instead of handing me the much-needed sixty dollars, I was told they would enter me in next month's drawing. Wait, what?! A drawing? I needed money now! I walked away very sad, knowing I wasn't going to be able to buy the feminine hygiene products I needed. So, what did I do? I went home to fashion a do-it-yourself, completely uncomfortable, and humbling temporary solution.

Thankfully, as luck would have it, the following month, I won the drawing and got the sixty bucks. I promptly went to the store and bought my very own tampons and discovered they aren't that expensive. Three life lessons learned: Don't be shy about learning the truth, even if it might be a little embarrassing. Financial security really matters. Providing for yourself solves a lot of problems.

For the next year, I worked hard at McDonald's and made myself as valuable an employee as I could be. I earned the respect of the crew. I showed up for optional training so I could better learn each part of the business. I worked longer hours in the summer. I gave it my all to be the best employee McDonald's had ever seen. Kelli, our general manager, intimidated me big time. She had such an air of authority that I wouldn't dare talk with her. Kelli likely had no idea how I was inspired to be just like her. I wanted to make her proud, and I wanted her to like me.

Like all teenagers, I was still discovering who I was. I mean, school was school, friends were friends, but where did I fit in? Kelli was my role model, mentor, and eventually my very good friend. But first, Kelli was my boss who promoted me to the drive-thru, and that made her the coolest person on the planet. How much did I respect Kelli? One day she told me wearing my black polyester McDonald's uniform pants with those white socks with the pink letters was tacky. From that day on,

I wore black socks. Years later, I bought my kids black socks, distinctly remembering that I didn't want my own kids to be "tacky." Oh, the things that stick to the teenage brain.

All my hard work didn't go without notice. In fact, I'd become a hot commodity on the fast-food burger circuit.

Burger King sat high on a hill near the McDonald's. As we know, BK is a direct competitor, and in Rifle, it wasn't uncommon for employees to be recruited between the two restaurants. BK offered me twenty-five cents more per hour to head up the hill, and I took it when McDonald's wouldn't match the offer. Have it your way, right? Every penny counted at my house, so an extra quarter an hour was something I couldn't afford to pass up. Besides, Burger King would allow me to ditch the polyester pants in favor of yoga pants. When you're sixteen, this sort of thing is a priority, and I had my priorities straight! BK assigned me to the drive-thru, and as I looked down at McDonald's, I raced to beat their drive-thru delivery times.

My tenure at BK didn't last long. Their culture was much more laid-back than at McDonald's—at least in Rifle. I encouraged my coworkers to step up their game, but the BK leadership was mellow and without the same drive and expectations Kelli had. I just couldn't work in an environment like that, so I met up with Kelli over lunch, and she hired me back—but with a raise. Looking back on it, I recognize that Kelli was allowing me to grow and learn things on my own. It was a wise move on her part because learning through living ended up being way more effective than trying to give a teenager advice and expecting them to listen.

Kelli was tough but fair. She had to suspend me from the drive-thru one summer after a customer complained when I tied my work shirt above my stomach—hey, I had to show off my summer tan! Evidently,

Kelli felt my bare waist was neither proper nor professional. There was also the time I confided in her that I felt bloated. Kelli told me I might need to "fart it out." That was Kelli—funny, strict, caring, successful, and an amazing role model to all of us.

Life at McDonald's was pretty good—maybe too good. By the time I was a senior, at age eighteen, I didn't care about a diploma, and I had zero interest in going to college. I loved my job. I reckoned that since Kelli had started working at McDonald's as a teenager and was now, in her thirties, making six figures a year, why would I want to do anything else? Heck, McDonald's offered me a shift manager position that paid more than $40,000 a year, and I was just a teenager. The choice between a high school geography class and a high-paying job, one that would put food on the table, was an easy one. I dropped out of high school and took the job.

This new gig was my element—taking care of customers, counting the drawers, managing food costs, setting the schedule, and making a difference. I started taking management training classes, and there was even talk about me going to Hamburger University, McDonald's management training center. I was valued and took pride in my job. The McDonald's in Rifle was my new home away from home.

Mom was devastated that I dropped out of high school. She, too, was a high school dropout and didn't want me to repeat her mistakes. She did everything she could to emphasize the importance of education as I grew up, and she felt like she'd failed. She also believed I was giving up on my future.

I was determined to prove her wrong. It was a strange dynamic between the pride of giving Mom most of my paychecks and then seeing her frustrated by my choices. Now that I'm a mother myself, I understand completely where she was coming from. Mom loved me and wanted the absolute best for her little girl.

I'd later earn a GED, and obviously, I didn't make a career at McDonald's after all. To this day, Kelli remains a great friend. She manages multiple McDonald's locations. She's a bright reflection of the opportunity McDonald's has created for so many Americans.

We need to put a greater emphasis on the value of teenagers finding meaningful work. We also need to break down the barriers to finding those jobs. Our country's teenage unemployment rate is often higher than overall unemployment. There is a real opportunity, often missed, to lay a solid foundation for the future for these teens. Real-life skills, a sense of accomplishment, and productivity are things everyone could use.

On the campaign trail, I often remarked that my first job at McDonald's changed my life. It set the foundation for a life filled with the dignity of work, self-reliance, and challenging myself to be the best at whatever I set my hand to. It also taught me that I could take better care of myself than the government ever could.

I flipped burgers, and I'm proud of that.

Thank you, McDonald's.

★ ★ ★

MARRIAGE, MOTHERHOOD, & MINISTRY

★ ★ ★

CHAPTER 5

Love at First Sight

I had a great run at working in fast food, but a lifelong career there just wasn't the plan for me. Though the experience proved life-changing, something—or I should say, "someone"—came along and even more profoundly changed it. One day, while on the tail end of my tenure at Burger King, a group of oil and gas roughnecks came in for lunch. It was the stereotypical group of young, tough, and hungry guys who were a little too loud and too flirtatious to get anywhere with their big talk. I could recognize most of these guys. They were harmless, although they likely annoyed the other customers just trying to enjoy their lunch. These young bucks seemed mostly concerned with making sure their buddies had a good laugh. I smiled but wasn't particularly interested in any of them.

Except one.

There was a new member of this crew who happened to be the most beautiful man I'd ever seen—not just in little Rifle, Colorado, but anywhere. He wasn't paying any attention to me at all. Instead, he was on his phone, wasn't flirting, wasn't being loud. This tall, dark, and handsome guy was different from the others, and he was ignoring me! Well, that just wasn't acceptable. He wasn't even trying, and he had my full attention. Just who was he?

Then it happened.

Hollywood couldn't have scripted it better. Like a moment straight from a movie—you know, where the man among the men delivers the perfect line, and the gal goes weak at the knees—this dreamy, rugged stud approached and calmly, confidently, and directly asked me, "What are we doing later?"

From that moment, Jayson Boebert and I have been together.

He just took my breath away. I fell in love with Jayson immediately, and I knew, without doubt, that he was the man I was meant to be with—for better or worse—forever. Oh, there'd be no stopping us. Marriage, kids, disagreements, fights, dreams, passion, love, faith, life— whatever was next—we were going to be together. We knew it. Even my mother, after she saw the two of us together, knew it.

Whatever life threw at Jayson and me, we'd figure it out—and there'd be a lot to figure out—beginning with telling him I was only sixteen. In fairness, Jayson, who was twenty-two, had no reason to believe I was that young, and at first, I was in no rush to tell him. Once I revealed my age, and after having had a chat with Mom about it, I reassured Jayson that everything was all right. Mom gave us her blessing, mainly because she trusted me. For any "Karen" who may be reading this, Jayson and I broke no Colorado laws with our relationship, despite what you might be thinking.

The more I got to know Jayson, the more in love with him I became. This hunky guy was new to Colorado, having just moved from his hometown of Las Vegas, Nevada, to work on a natural gas drilling rig. He'd worked his entire adult life in the oil and gas fields.

Jayson came to Colorado because, in Vegas, he was unemployed, homeless, and in dire need of changing the direction of his life. He'd been getting into trouble and walking a path he knew he wasn't likely to survive. Jayson's buddy found work in western Colorado, where the natural gas drilling business was in high gear, so Jayson packed what few things he had into a trash bag and hitched a ride for the seven-hour drive to Grand Junction. After a few days of trying and failing to find work there, he made his way fifty miles further east to Rulison, a blip of a community alongside Interstate 70. It's best known as the site of Project Rulison, where in 1969, a forty-three-kiloton nuclear bomb was detonated underground to free up large amounts of natural gas. Rulison was now home to a man camp for Nabors Drilling, a subsidiary of Nabors Industries—one of the largest oil and gas drilling companies in the world. For those who might not know, "man camp" is a nifty term for temporary housing for oil field workers.

That man camp looked pretty darn good to Jayson. Here was a guy who had nowhere to sleep, was basically broke, and still unemployed. If the word "gumption" had a face, it'd be Jayson. He decided to act like he was supposed to be at that man camp and grabbed a bunk. Fake it 'til you make it, I guess. He told anyone who asked that he was being hired on. As far as Jayson was concerned, Nabors Drilling was hiring him; they just didn't know it yet. After a couple of days, he finally met up with a Nabors district manager who saw how hungry Jayson was for work and agreed to give him a shot. The company hired him to do grunt work—basically doing maintenance and cleaning around the rig. Jayson also connected pipes together so the rig could push down another thirty feet deep, a process that seemed never-ending, and he couldn't have been more appreciative of the opportunity.

The turnover rate was high for those drilling company workers—many of the new crew members who were initially attracted to the high pay found this work and lifestyle too challenging. Some either took jobs elsewhere, quit, or they just plain stopped showing up. You really needed to love the work to stay there. The good news for Jayson was with all the attrition, an intelligent, hard worker like him moved up the ranks quickly.

This was the go-getter I'd met at Burger King.

Our relationship moved quickly from there. As Billy Crystal says in the timeless romantic comedy, *When Harry Met Sally*, "When you realize you want to spend the rest of your life with somebody, you want that the rest of your life start as soon as possible." So, four months after we met, Jayson and I went off to get married.

Mom rode with us to Vegas, where we planned to marry in a little white wedding chapel. Literally, it's called "A Little White Wedding Chapel," a Vegas institution that's got a drive-thru wedding window for couples really in a hurry. While we didn't feel the need for that, the chapel did offer a variety of wedding packages. Want Elvis to officiate? You got it. Want to get married while sitting in a classic pink Cadillac? They've got that too. When we showed up, the chapel also offered up a Britney Spears package—that's the one I convinced Jayson we needed, and we agreed upon, though to this day, and likely until the day he dies, he insists we ordered the Michael Jordan special. In the end, it didn't really matter because, as we learned there at the chapel, we couldn't get married until I turned seventeen. So, Jayson and I spent the weekend with family and celebrated our marriage but without the actual marriage.

Even though it wasn't yet official, Jayson and I felt like husband and wife. Our families felt that way too. I couldn't have been happier.

A lot of people would say we moved way too fast, but we didn't think that at all. Make no mistake: this was no shotgun wedding. Jayson and I intentionally wanted to get married and start our new life together. I had complete faith he was the man I was supposed to be with, and there was no changing my mind. As far as I was concerned, there was no reason to wait. My dream in life was to be a loving mom and a good wife.

We had a common-law marriage until I was almost twenty-one, but since a common-law marriage isn't sufficient for some insurance purposes, we got officially married in 2007.

Now that I'm a public figure, my marriage to Jayson and our history together has often been the source of attacks from the Democrats. It's not lost on me that they should actually be celebrating us for overcoming a lot of life's obstacles. But it's also not lost on me that our path doesn't follow the script for well-to-do country club Republicans, either. We were certainly young and feisty and broke the mold for a typical conservative couple. It's how I grew up, and it's my life. I'm darn proud of my family and our four boys.

That, of course, makes no difference to your political opponents. They'll do anything and everything to gin up the politics of personal destruction. For example, take the night Jayson decided to try to bond with my stepfather. The two of them went to the Rifle bowling alley and got to chatting over drinks. The female bartender flirted with Jayson, having heard previously from his friends what a catch he'd be. They even teased her by saying he'd gotten a great tattoo in a private area, which made her curious, so she pressed Jayson to show it to her right there at the bar. He ignored her and was embarrassed she was doing it in front of my stepfather.

She wouldn't stop.

Jayson, clearly having had too much to drink, decided he'd heard enough, stood up, and acted like he was going to unzip his pants. Before he got that far, the owner of the bowling alley intervened. He told Jayson to stop and kicked him out. Jayson felt he was the one being harassed and didn't want to leave. The two argued, and Jayson threw a basket of fries at the owner. The police were called.

The bartender told officers Jayson exposed himself, which he vehemently denied, both then and now. It also turned out that the bartender was only seventeen, which made it illegal for her to be working as a bartender in the first place. No one could have known she wasn't an adult. Nevertheless, Jayson was arrested for indecent exposure to a minor.

He was a young oil field worker without a lawyer or the desire to hire one. Instead of fighting for his innocence in court, Jayson took a plea deal, which resulted in him having a permanent criminal record. At the time, it didn't matter to Jayson that he was pleading guilty. He knew the truth—and the truth was, he didn't do what he was accused of. But the entire experience opened Jayson's eyes to the reality that he needed the alcohol and anger management classes that came with the plea deal. For someone with no childhood role models or guidance, those classes were immeasurably helpful in teaching him how to make better choices.

Fast-forward a couple of decades, and now that I'm in the public eye, the Left attacks us relentlessly—facts be damned. They point to Jayson's arrest and say awful things about him—rather than applaud a man who's made a few mistakes along the way, learned from them, and then made himself a true success, got married, and is raising four incredible young men.

Meanwhile, CNN has a contributor who got caught masturbating on a Zoom call with his colleagues, and the Left goes silent.

Go figure.

★ ★ ★ CHAPTER 6 ★ ★ ★

Working in the Gas Patch

When Jayson and I first got together, I was still working for McDonald's—fortunately with a schedule that gave me the flexibility to visit him at the rig. I liked keeping him company and would often bring a meal for us to eat together. The time I spent out there introduced me to an industry most people never get a chance to experience. Before I met Jayson, I never gave much thought to how the natural gas we use to heat our homes is produced. Now, I found myself in a front-row seat watching the back-breaking work that benefits all of us.

During my early visits to the rig, I'd stay in the "doghouse"—the part of the rig that served as the drillers' cabin and looked a lot like a shipping container. Sometimes I'd go out in the middle of the night to help Jayson make pipe connections. It was great to be a part of it, and I got the added benefit of getting to spend more time with my man.

The work isn't for everyone. This is a male-dominated industry for good reason. It's physical and pushes people to their limits. The rigs worked twenty-four-seven, no matter what the temperature was outside, no matter how much snow was falling, and no matter how windy or miserable it got. If your life wasn't in danger, you worked. It probably wouldn't be anywhere on the list of dream jobs for most people, but Jayson loved it, and I loved what he and his crew were capable of doing every day. Man, they worked long hours, but they had swagger and a real sense of pride about what they did for a living.

Their attitude wasn't much different from mine at McDonald's—I, too, was proud of the work I did. But with all the time I was spending out at the gas patch with Jayson, the energy workers I'd befriended encouraged me to try to get hired on too. They knew I liked it out there and wanted to be a part of it. I seriously considered what they were saying. So after a few sleepless nights, I decided it was time to leave McDonald's. It was bittersweet. Kelli had become more than my boss; she was now my friend. And McDonald's was my first-ever job—and a transformative one at that. But the decision was made. I was now off to join the energy industry.

It's not every day someone makes the move from burgers to natural gas, although I'm sure there's a digestive joke in there somewhere. But I've said a million times that McDonald's taught me many handy skills, and I applied those skills at my new job—office work with one of the largest natural gas producers in America, at their gas processing plant in the nearby town of Parachute. The company is a part of a multi-billion-dollar energy company started by a couple of hard-working brothers more than a hundred years ago.

Life was moving along fast. After living lean and trying to save a few bucks along the way, Jayson and I decided it was time to rent a place for ourselves. The following summer, we also decided to start a family, and in 2005, our first son, Tyler, was born. I left high school then to take the management position at McDonald's. By 2006, I was working in the gas patch. I was now officially a working mother, and I loved both jobs—the one at home and the one at the office.

The upside to having spent time with Jayson in the gas fields was that what I learned out there helped me in the office. I knew what the reports meant, why they were needed, and why we needed to be able to access them. I understood it all better than most of my office coworkers. I never could have known that all the days I'd spend hanging out with Jayson would turn out to be great on-the-job training!

I'd been at my office job for about a year when my best friend there told me she'd decided to take a job in the drilling department. That meant I wouldn't be spending my days with her, which saddened me but also made me think about what I really wanted to do. If I was being truly honest with myself, I had the urge to work in the field. Heck, I liked the idea of working outdoors and driving a company truck, with the added benefits of a company phone and computer. Oh, and it paid more money. I especially liked the thought of that.

The head of the pipeline department was the one I needed to see, so I went over and asked whether there were opportunities for fieldwork. He said there were but expressed concern I might not be able to hold my own against the guys out there. To convince him otherwise, I told him I'd work a week for free to prove I could do it. He agreed to let me. So, for one week, I rode around in a truck, shadowing the team and learning how to be a pumper—an entry-level position where one learns the production side of the business.

When the drilling rig, where Jayson worked, and the completions rig—the fracking—do their jobs, the production crew then comes in to extract the gas from the well. From there, it goes to the midstream units for distribution. In other words, a steel pipe goes into the ground, the pipe is stimulated, and then they get it flowing. A pumper maintains the well location (the wellheads, the separator unit, the flow lines, the battery tanks). Their job includes power washing, changing plungers in the wellhead, and other regular maintenance. Pumpers check the wells they oversee and identify problems if anything is offline.

After that paycheck-free week of following the pumper around, I went back to talk with the head of the pipeline department. I knew I'd held my own against the guys and was convinced I'd do an excellent job if he hired me. I walked into his office and made it clear I was ready to be a pumper. He looked at me, smiled, and told me he already had a job for me, one that would be an even better fit.

Looking back, I think the guy was just testing me that first week. He wanted to see what kind of mettle I had—if I'd work hard and be dependable. I passed the test, and he hired me into the department. I was now a pipeline locator.

At the time, a lot of the field maps were outdated, so my job was to find all the pipelines in their operation. To do that, I'd drive my truck into the field and track the pipe locations via GPS, then download the data back to the office where the maps were updated. It was like a surveying job. The work could be a bit tedious but was not without some great benefits—I spent time in the beautiful countryside, hiked up and down mountains, and enjoyed the time outside.

The company clearly believed in me because they sent me to classes to learn how to manage the cathodic pipe protection systems—a low voltage corrosion control system that helps protect the pipe. I'd test the pipe, and if this low voltage protection wasn't installed or wasn't working, then we'd take a crew out to fix the issue.

Too often, the corrosion protection wasn't working because the roughnecks on the drilling rigs would turn off the anodes, which interfered with their drilling tools. Those anodes are vital to supplying the direct electrochemical current needed to protect the pipe from corrosion, so it was a problem when they were switched off. It happened often enough that I stayed fairly busy sorting it all out with the crews. Nevertheless, I loved my work and everything that came with it. I wore steel-toed boots, fire retardant clothing, and a pink hard hat. I had a company truck, a company computer, and a company phone. The company appreciated me, Jayson was proud of me, and I was proud of me. I'd made a good go of it in the gas patch.

Being part of a team was also important to me. I worked with a fun group of people who just loved messing with me for their own enjoyment. Early on, they'd send me to the parts store with an extensive list of equipment to buy. It would include things like a skyhook and a pipe stretcher. They made it clear I wasn't supposed to come back without these parts. The problem, of course, is there are no such things as a skyhook or a pipe stretcher.

Boom! Roasted!

I worked for the energy company up until the day before I delivered our second son, Brody. I'm sure Pete Buttigieg will be disappointed, but I didn't stay on parental leave for long. Four weeks later, I decided it was time to get back to work because I missed it, missed the people, and most of all, I missed the pride of earning my own paycheck.

Even out at the gas patch, I was able to find a good babysitter, and we fell into a nice rhythm. I'd wake up at 4:00 a.m. to nurse Brody and fill up his bottles for the day. Then I'd put together enough food to last the sitter and Tyler the entire day. From there, I'd pile us all in the truck and head over to the sitter's house. After dropping off the kids, I'd have just enough time to get to work by 5:30 a.m.

Life went like that for another couple of years, but when I got pregnant with my third child, Kaydon, it was time to call it quits. That's when Jayson and I decided I would leave the gas patch to become a full-time, stay-at-home mom. This was 2008. As the economy started tanking, Colorado's politicians went on an anti-fossil fuel march, and people in the energy industry were powerless to stop forced pay cuts or their jobs from being eliminated. I figured this was a good time to stay at home with my kids.

The time I spent in the gas patch was one of the most rewarding of my life. I made lifelong friends and saw firsthand the commitment those workers make to responsibly develop our natural resources. In fact, former pad sites have been completely restored to their natural state. If you believed the liberal environmentalists, you'd think energy workers leave those sites as scorched earth.

There were lessons learned in those fields, not the least of which is just how important those local energy jobs are to hard-working Americans. They put food on the table and improve lives. It's merit-based work, where there's a reward for showing up on time, giving it your all, and making yourself valuable to your employer. The sad thing is, as I saw during my time in the gas patch, the heavy hand of the government can overregulate these people out of their jobs and ruin the local economy.

I'd have a little something to say about all that one day—on the campaign trail and then again as a member of the House Committee on Natural Resources.

CHAPTER 7

Foreclosure

In my early twenties, I had always managed to earn enough to pay cash for my needs. But I'd never made a major purchase and never started establishing credit. By his early twenties, Jayson had admittedly been financially irresponsible. He'd missed enough payments that his credit score wasn't good. Jayson and I were both earning good paychecks, so we did make a sound financial decision—to stop renting and instead buy a home for our family. But Jayson's bad credit hurt our chances of getting a loan, and my having no credit made it even less likely.

The bank made it clear we were not the poster couple for lending success, so Jayson and I got to work repairing and establishing credit. This was a painstaking process that took some time. But we ultimately improved our credit scores. Between those improved scores and the money we'd saved for a down payment, by 2007, we were ready to go. Given our financial history, we'd have to pay a far higher interest rate, but it was time to live the American Dream and become homeowners.

With the energy industry humming along, cash flowing from our jobs, and a strong local real estate market, we bought our first home.

But those years with less than stellar credit came back to rear their ugly head, and we overpaid in every way—the purchase price, the loan at 10 percent interest, and a mortgage insurance payment of $800 a month. Sure, we overpaid, but it didn't matter to us at the time. We could afford the payments, and we just knew we would live there forever.

For the next couple of years, we truly loved our home. We invested in upgrades, remodeled it, cared for it, and were so proud to live in it. We had plenty of room, and the house sat on acreage in the country, where we enjoyed the outdoors, and the kids had plenty of space to play.

In 2009, our economic world was rocked, right alongside millions of Americans. Jayson's earnings were cut back significantly, along with all of his coworkers who were struggling to make things work. The writing was on the wall for my job, too, but I was pregnant, and we had already decided it was time to focus on being a full-time mom.

Every day, news reports flooded the airwaves about the national financial crisis and how people were at risk of losing their homes. Home valuations were dropping like a rock. People were abandoning their mortgages left and right, some far before they had to. The government and banks were introducing ways to renegotiate mortgages so that people didn't lose their homes. Unemployment rates skyrocketed. Things were ugly all the way around for lots of people in our situation.

As the situation worsened, Jayson and I regrouped. It became clear that as hard as we worked, it was going to be very difficult to make our mortgage and truck payments and still meet all of our family's needs. We may have both been determined to make it through the crisis without help, but it was clear we were at risk of losing everything. I called our mortgage company and asked if we could talk about ways to modify our loan so we could afford it. The representative immediately said Jayson and I weren't eligible for a mortgage modification because we hadn't missed a payment. I explained how we didn't want to miss a payment because we preferred not to destroy the credit we'd worked so hard to fix. I was told it didn't matter; I would need to miss a payment before they could investigate it. That made absolutely no sense. I called everyone else at the mortgage company, and I'd tell anyone who would take my call the same thing.

Jayson and I thought long and hard about the situation and what the mortgage company told us. So, with great consternation, we ultimately decided to skip a payment. We still set aside the money we would have otherwise paid and saved it. I called the mortgage company again. This time, they said we'd need to miss two payments. Again, I tried explaining our situation to anyone who would listen, because this didn't sound right to me at all. Again, they told me they couldn't do anything without us being behind two payments.

So, we again skipped a payment.

We still put the money aside that we would have used for that payment. The money for both missed payments was in a savings account. Now that we were two months behind—following the mortgage company's instructions—I called them back and unbelievably got the runaround yet again. This was a never-ending series of unreturned phone calls and then inconsistent messages. Now they were telling us they couldn't begin working to restructure our mortgage until ninety days after a missed payment.

I felt completely lost and helpless. No one at that company would help. It was beyond stressful, and now a feeling of hopelessness began sinking in.

A third payment was "missed" and set aside. I called the mortgage company again. They said there was nothing I could do because the property was now in foreclosure. I asked what options we had to fix the problem—their answer? The bank would repossess the house, and we'd be booted out of it. Two months later, they did just that.

We lost our home despite the fact that Congress had authorized billions of dollars for loan modifications to help people in our exact situation. This was one of the saddest times our family, to this day, has ever experienced. The feeling was only made worse when the bank put our house up for sale at nearly half the price we'd paid.

It didn't matter that we tried to help solve the problem. It didn't matter that we had the money to make the mortgage payment. We lost our home, just like so many other people. We didn't make excuses. And as hard as it was, we moved on.

Now we had to find a home to rent, and that's not always easy, especially when so many others are navigating similar challenges. Besides, we had two dogs, three kids, and a ton of stuff from living on a huge plot of land in the country. Hey, neighbors, watch out! Here come the Clampetts!

We found a place to rent, and for the next ten years, we made cash payments. The security deposits, first and last month's rent, we paid in cash. Later, when we started a restaurant, we paid cash to remodel the building. We paid cash to open it. The mortgage nightmare meant credit wasn't an option. Heck, we didn't have the desire to pursue credit at this point anyway. Jayson and I decided that nobody would take anything from us again. Ever. We had zero faith that the "system" would work for us and wanted nothing to do with it. We would earn and pay for what we needed all by ourselves.

In 2015, journalist David Dayen wrote an article for *The Intercept* titled, "Obama Program That Hurt Homeowners and Helped Big

Banks is Ending."[1] The sub-headline said it all: "The Home Affordable Modification Program (HAMP) was supposed to help millions of homeowners avoid foreclosure. It didn't." Dayen noted how the laws resulted in doing more to make people lose faith in progressive government solutions than anything the programs ever accomplished. He explained how the mortgage companies didn't have the incentives to help people, that instead, they made a ton of money in the accumulated fees that were racked up when they strung out the modification process for months. It turned out foreclosure was a better outcome for those mortgage companies. They had no desire to help anybody but themselves. More than 70 percent of the people who applied for relief were turned down. Jayson and I didn't even get to the application process.

Dayen concluded with this—and it's almost as if he'd been there with Jayson and me because it was so accurate: "Families who sought out a government program to assist them in a time of need saw only a mortgage servicer who lost their paperwork, strung along their requests, and injured their financial security. The millions who experienced this abuse will find it difficult to ever believe in government again."

Is it any wonder?

I've often said I'm a self-taught conservative whose life experiences formed my conservative principles. Put this foreclosure in that bucket.

Was it painful to lose our family home?

Yes.

Did I have a role in all of this, and am I more cautious because of this experience? Yes.

Did the government's policies play a role in the economic downturn that would eventually cost our jobs and our home?

---

[1] Dayen, David. "Obama Program That Hurt Homeowners and Helped Big Banks is Ending." *The Intercept* December 28, 2015

Yes.

Would my personal experience affect my thinking about the proper role of government? Yes.

Would I have done something else with a better understanding of what the outcome would have been?

Maybe.

Would I trust the government to effectively address another crisis like this, say, for a pandemic?

Absolutely not.

★ ★ ★ CHAPTER 8 ★ ★ ★

Highway Delivery

Jayson and I had quite the growing family. We had been blessed with three strapping boys—Tyler, Brody, and Kaydon—when God decided to bless us with a fourth, our son, Roman. As I'm writing this, our sons range in age from nine to sixteen years old.

As parents, Jayson and I are making a conscious effort to raise our boys to grow into strong, independent men. Their success will come from faith, family, respect, and hard work, and not from entitlement, safe spaces, or the government. We're bringing them up on a rural country farm, where they spend plenty of time exploring and playing outside and taking care of our dogs, chickens, goats, and whatever other random animals they've dragged into the house. They're "boy's boys"—getting a kick out of things like mud, motorcycles, and such.

Tyler, Brody, Kaydon, and Roman mean the world to me. They're my life, and I want them to know a future in the same incredible country I know. I believe parents have a mandate to secure a good future for their children, and I took that mandate with me to Washington. If we don't fight for this country, what kind of place will it be when our children grow up? But to fight the good fight for their future and the future of America, at least in my household, means my boys won't always have a typical childhood. I mean, I must split time between Washington and our home in Colorado. The good news is that they're supportive of my decision to pursue public service. They know why I'm in Congress and the sacrifices that go with it. Each of them knows I want a bright future for them, one that's full of opportunity, and that I'm working hard toward that end. Jayson and I have dedicated ourselves to building a foundation of faith and love for those boys, and it has served us well.

Experiencing a miscarriage and four full-term pregnancies opened my eyes to many things. For one, along with my Christian beliefs, I became more resolute in my pro-life stance. Also, the way in which each of my children came into the world helped me see firsthand the health insurance challenges faced by so many Americans every day.

With my first two sons, the doctor induced labor, and their delivery was drama-free. Tyler, our oldest, was seven pounds, three ounces, and Brody was six pounds, twelve ounces. Thankfully, both were healthy, beautiful babies. But my third delivery was one you just had to see to believe—and trust me: there's a Colorado cop who probably wishes he hadn't! This delivery ended up making the local newspaper because, well, sometimes the truth is way stranger than fiction!

I was more than nine months into my pregnancy, forty weeks to be exact, and as any mom can imagine, I was more than ready for this baby to come out. Though it lasted a little longer than my others, this pregnancy seemed on track to be just as routine—until it wasn't. While I was decidedly ready for Kaydon to come out, I was not ready for just how fast he chose to do so!

A little after midnight, I was awakened by consistent contractions. I rolled over and told Jayson, but he wasn't panicked at all. He went back to sleep. Not me, though. I climbed out of bed and called my midwife at the hospital. The contractions were mild but consistent, so she and I decided I'd wait an hour and then head to the hospital, which was twenty miles away.

Now that I think about it clearly, we should have left earlier, but honestly, at that moment, there was no way of knowing what a difference an hour would make. Trust me: it would have been huge. Besides, I wanted time to make myself more presentable for our "mom and baby" pictures.

With my first two sons, the pictures weren't that great. I mean, the babies looked amazing, but me, not so much. With both boys, the doctor induced delivery. That's great for convenience in that we know ahead of time when the baby is coming. There's no hurried or late-night birth, and everyone, from the doctors to family and friends, is prepared. However, it did mean a labor that lasted from eight to ten hours, after which I looked far less than my best. This time, I was determined not to let that happen. So, I showered, fixed my hair and makeup, and an hour later, I woke Jayson up (again) to tell him I was ready to leave for the hospital. Then I went to our guest bedroom to wake up Jayson's mom, who was visiting in anticipation of her grandchild's birth. I told her what was going on and asked that she watch Tyler and Brody. I figured this was better than dragging everyone to the hospital in the middle of the night, especially since I anticipated hours of labor.

The contractions were getting stronger, so I went to get Jayson. He was back in bed! Men. I let him know rather sternly that it really was time to go. He reluctantly got ready. I left the keys to our newer and nicer family truck on the counter so my mother-in-law could drive the kids to meet us later in the morning. Jayson and I hopped into our older Ford F-250—Jayson's old and dirty gas patch work truck—and left for the hospital. I only mention this because if you're not in a clean vehicle, well, any expectant mother would be horrified by what happened next.

We left for the hospital, and although I was giddy with excitement, I was also concerned that my contractions were becoming increasingly aggressive. God bless Jayson, but we had twenty miles to go, the roads were empty in the middle of the night, and he was driving like an old lady. Maybe I should have driven. After all, I am the faster driver. Jayson's a chill guy behind the wheel. Typically, he'll play some country music and enjoy the ride. But tonight? Could he at least drive the speed limit?!

Five minutes into the drive, I started to panic. I knew we weren't going to make it to the hospital in time. The contractions were crazy strong. I told Jayson to speed up, and I wasn't being diplomatic. I knew he thought I was overreacting and was sure we had a long, long labor ahead, just like before. But I knew better. I moved my feet up onto the seat and squatted, one hand on the center seat console, the other on the door.

My water broke.

That certainly got Jayson's attention! Finally, he put the pedal to the metal.

We were flying down the empty interstate at over eighty miles per hour, but even then, I knew we weren't going to make it in time. I told Jayson I was pushing, and he told me to stop. I told him I couldn't stop because my body was pushing, and I couldn't control it. He pressed the accelerator as hard as it would go. Too late. The baby's head popped out. Was this really happening? Yep, right there in the truck, at over one hundred miles per hour just outside of Glenwood Springs.

My seat-squatting technique was exhausting, so I moved to sit up on the center console with my pants pulled down. I faced out toward the passenger window while my newborn child was starting to make his way into the world. If you're questioning the safety of this maneuver, I agree with you. Jayson told me to hang on, that he was going to pull over to help, but as soon as he hit the exit ramp, I had another strong contraction. Yep, Kaydon had no intention of waiting any longer.

I moved back to my seat-squatting position and let gravity take over. It may not have been pretty, it may not have been classy, but it still got the job done. Kaydon Boebert, our biggest baby yet at just over eight pounds, was officially born at 2:09 a.m. in the front cab of our Ford F-250 pickup truck on an Interstate 70 off-ramp. I scooped our wonderful little baby boy up into my arms as Jayson was pulling over and said, "Don't stop now. Let's get to the hospital!"

When we got back onto the road, our little boy wasn't making any noise. Did I need to spank his little bottom? Or was that just something doctors do on TV? Jayson told me to try it. I didn't want to hurt Kaydon, so I lightly tapped his slippery yet adorable tiny bottom. Nothing happened. I tried a little harder tap, and he started to make a little noise. That was enough for me. Big sigh of relief.

We were doing fifty miles per hour in a twenty-five-mph zone on an empty Grand Avenue at two in the morning, just minutes from the hospital. Then, there it was, out of nowhere—a police car with its lights and sirens full tilt pulling up behind us.

Really? Now?

At that moment, you could've just called us "Bonnie" and "Clyde" because there was no way on God's great earth we were pulling over. I called 911 and explained that I'd just given birth in my truck and was headed for the hospital. The dispatcher contacted the police officer, explained the situation, and then told us to keep driving and that the officer would follow us. Hmm, that sure sounded like permission to hit the gas.

We were quite the sight to behold as Jayson pulled into the emergency room entrance. The police officer ran around to the passenger door to see me in all my glory, baby in hand. The umbilical cord was still attached, so it was awkward when Jayson picked me up and carried us inside. As I cradled my baby, the officer escorted us down a long hall toward the end of the emergency room. I can't even imagine how we looked to everyone inside! They looked beyond freaked out, but I was happy and calm. I just knew everything would be all right and that someday this would make for a fine story. In fact, the local newspaper did a write-up about our little adventure. It makes me smile knowing Kaydon has that article, which he can one day share with his own kids, about the day he was born.

A nurse wheeled me up to the delivery room, where I was met by my hospital midwife. Later, I'd call the billing department, and after explaining all that had happened, I was able to negotiate a 50 percent discount. It certainly didn't seem right to pay the full rate for a job that nature and I did all on our own out on the interstate.

The entire experience was a good reminder that if we stand on faith, especially when life takes an unexpected turn, things do turn out all right in the end.

CHAPTER 9

Birthing Babies & Goats

The adventure of delivering Kaydon led to quite a bit of reflection when the time came to deliver Roman. I thought quite a bit about my previous three deliveries, and after considering the advice of friends who'd also had previous delivery complications, I concluded I'd give birth at home. After everything I'd been through before, I figured a home delivery would be much, much easier. Plus, there was the bonus of preventing a late-night truck race to the hospital.

Life was great. We were fortunate enough to be in a financial position that allowed me to be a stay-at-home mom. But the finances would change for the worse during the seventh month of my pregnancy. President Obama and the state of Colorado were pushing tighter oil and gas regulations, which were having their intended effect of slowing energy production. Their decisions hit home when Jayson found himself out of work and without insurance. Our local economy was tanking. Nobody was hiring. And while we had some savings, we were going to be depending on what we had set aside to get us through a tough time.

The situation wasn't a good one. Like so many others, our livelihood was directly impacted by decisions the government made—and the people in charge didn't seem to care how their decisions affected hard-working Americans. All of this eventually helped me to better understand the health insurance challenges faced by so many people across the country. As good fortune would have it, giving birth at home with a midwife was far more affordable than the alternative of going to the hospital.

Roman's delivery turned out to be an amazing life experience that I wouldn't trade for anything. As much as I'd planned for the delivery itself, I'd also given a lot of thought to the overall experience, not just for me, but for the rest of the family. I wanted this birth to be a family affair, one filled with the same joy and love I'd experienced with the birth of our previous three children, with Jayson, Mom, and Jayson's mother right there by my side.

As God and nature intended, in the ninth month, Roman decided it was time. One morning I woke up with contractions and called my birth midwife. After talking through what I was feeling, she made her way toward the house. I still figured it would be all day until the baby arrived.

Finally, I had the time to prepare for a delivery.

I was told to move around, maybe walk some stairs. As I did, I thought about what would happen later that day and had reservations about Brody seeing the birth. He was just too young, and I decided it would be better for him to go to school—and I'd go with him. I climbed on my bicycle, he got on his, and we rode side-by-side to school. It wasn't that far, and since I'd already given birth by a roadside, I figured it'd be okay to take a bike ride near my house. So there we were, a little boy and his nine-month pregnant mom riding bikes to school. I can only imagine what people were saying as we passed by or when I made my way back home by myself.

When I got back to the house, I was happy, dancing and singing and just basking in the joy of the day. When I had a strong contraction, I told Jayson the baby was getting close. He'd learned his lesson from the last delivery when he thought I was overreacting, and this time, he paid attention! Jayson told the midwife it was time to get this baby delivered. She argued it was too early for me to get into the bathtub. She also wasn't eager to check on me because doing so too often can put moms at risk of infection. Jayson pressed her to do it anyway, and it's a good thing he did. She saw I was already dilated ten centimeters and told Jayson to get the tub filled up immediately.

In the bathroom, there was a separate tub and shower, and it was a relatively small space. With the midwife at my side, I climbed into the tub filled with warm water. I was as comfortable as I could be in that situation, and given I'd been through three other deliveries, I knew, just by how my body felt, that this delivery was going to happen quickly.

In the days leading up to this moment, I'd made it clear I wanted the family to experience the birth with me, but I underestimated how literally they were going to take that. My mother-in-law, Mom, and Tyler stood inside the shower. Jayson, and our dog, Dozer, were in the doorway as Mom's friend, a two-year-old Kaydon, and his babysitter peered in from just outside the door. As if the audience wasn't large enough, Mom had family in Florida also watching on FaceTime. This was going to be quite the event.

As I soaked in the tub, I was a bit concerned that my water had yet to break and asked the midwife if I should try to break it myself. This caught the attention of Mom's friend, who swung the lens of her camcorder over to capture the action. I quickly put a stop to that. Can you imagine the media getting hold of footage like that now?

Once I'd entered the tub, I didn't have to stay there long. Within ten minutes, Roman Boebert was born. He was seven pounds, three ounces of pure happiness. I scooped him up to my chest, and everyone in that tiny, cramped bathroom had tears in their eyes. It was an absolutely beautiful moment. I was surrounded by the people I loved, sharing one of life's miracles in the comfort of my own home.

During my pregnancy, whenever I'd tell a girlfriend I was planning a home birth, they'd seem skeptical. I understood why, but now, having delivered two kids in a hospital, one in a pickup truck on the interstate, and one in a tub, I can truthfully say I wish I'd had all four at home. Roman's delivery was one of the most peaceful, loving, and beautiful moments of my life.

Dolly the Goat Gives Birth

I figured since Roman's birth at home wasn't such an ordeal, then it might also be a nice experience for my favorite pregnant goat.

Yep, that happened.

Dolly was only eleven days old when she first joined the Boebert family. A customer of Shooters had pitched giving me Dolly because she was cute and fun and was a fainting goat. A fainting goat! Of course, I was on board.

When a fainting goat gets excited about anything, even something as mundane as eating, its muscles seize to the point that it topples over. Then the goat will relax, get back up, and do it all again. It's quite entertaining. Search YouTube for "fainting goats," and you'll understand what I mean. Unfortunately, it didn't take long to find out that Dolly wasn't actually of the fainting breed, but she was still darn cute.

I'd nurse her with a milk bottle. Dolly would sit in the front seat of my car when I ran errands. She'd follow me everywhere and even managed to get Jayson and me to let her sleep at the foot of our bed. Dolly was even house-trained. I'd trained her to nudge the door when she needed to go outside to do her business.

As Dolly got older, she spent more time outside with our billy goat, who took a real liking to her. Obviously. One day, we realized Dolly was pregnant.

Now, I knew I'd be able to help Dolly with the birth of her baby because I'd helped cats and dogs give birth in the past, and I loved it. I watched videos on how to birth baby goats and learned the signs to look for. But Dolly's belly sure looked bigger than what I'd seen in the videos. Maybe there were a couple of goats hiding in that belly of hers? When Dolly wouldn't leave my side and seemed very needy, I knew her day had come.

I set up my bathroom with blankets, towels, hay, and water, and I brought Dolly in to get comfortable for the big moment. Like me, it didn't take long for that moment to arrive. About an hour after we entered the bathroom, Dolly went into labor, and she gave birth to two new baby goats, Dottie and Cash.

I cleaned up Dolly and her two kids and beamed with pride. Later that night, with a big smile on my face, I fell asleep right there on the bathroom floor alongside the three of them.

We were all fantastic. Isn't life great?

CHAPTER 10

Jailhouse Minister

By the end of 2009, I had been spending all my time as a stay-at-home mom. As much as I enjoyed the extra time, I also recognized I could put that time and energy toward something beyond the day-to-day routine I'd established.

What would that be? I'm at my best keeping busy, and I enjoy working, but with Jayson's erratic travel schedule and young kids to take care of, it was also important that I appreciate the blessing of spending time at home, which I did. I just needed to find something to add to the mix.

Then I learned the pastors at our church in Rifle were moving out of town, so I thought now was a good time to try a new church in nearby Glenwood Springs.

On the first Sunday of 2010, I made the half-hour drive with the kids over to our new church—a non-denominational, full gospel, Christian church. Something positive stirred in me. I suddenly felt a profound desire to be more involved in the church and to encourage my kids to be as well. I wanted to raise them with a strong commitment to Christianity, and as I thought about it, I realized that I, too, desired a closer relationship with God. I wanted to lead by example about the importance of church for the boys.

As I grew in my faith, my bible reading became more focused, and I couldn't wait to get to church. I made the commitment to rededicate my life to Jesus—to make Him the lord and master of my life and to allow Him to guide me in every area. This meant I got more involved with bible studies, prayer groups, and volunteer outreach events. As with most things in my life, I went all in. Whenever the church doors were open, I tried to be there. It was common for the boys and me to be in church five or six days a week.

I started attending prayer school, a thirty-six-week comprehensive and interactive program about the different types of prayer. It was designed to push everyone's envelope to truly explore their relationship with God. It was deep, meaningful, and effective. I attended bible school at the church, a one-day-per-week program that gave me a clearer understanding of Christianity. The lessons were taught by a fantastic pastor who'd developed an excellent reputation among his peers for his leadership and knowledge. I was like a sponge, just soaking up the lessons. As God often does, He sets you up for the future without you knowing it at the time. This pastor was giving me the education, knowledge, and process that I would later use to teach others.

Having now spent considerable time attending church, prayer school, and bible school, I was excited to share my knowledge and commitment to God with others. I'd been aware for a while that some of our church members volunteered for the church's jail ministry. They'd spend time at the local Garfield County jail sharing a message of faith with the inmates. This was a ministry I'd been wanting to get involved with but never felt confident to do so. I hadn't felt qualified to teach about things I was still learning myself. I thought, Who was I to preach to others?

One day, the leader of the jail ministry approached me and asked if I'd be interested in serving on the team. I really appreciated him asking, but I had doubts about my ability to be effective. He reassured me that I'd be able to contribute in a meaningful way. But there was another obstacle I needed to overcome. Typically, to be allowed to participate in the jail ministry, you had to have finished the two-year bible school program, but I was still in my first year. The ministry leader said he saw my commitment, enthusiasm, and desire, and he promised that if I agreed to join the team, he'd find a way forward. I think he saw me as a go-getter.

After being assured I could meaningfully contribute, I joined the ministry. There were a few things still to be done before I could share my faith at the jail, though. I had to be credentialed, which includes a background check, and takes about a month, plus I had to complete a county jail inmate volunteer training program. The program gives guidance on what you can and can't do when interacting with the inmates. While all of this seemed a bit overwhelming, I figured since the process took a month, I'd have time to think on whether this was something I could do. I decided to go for it and signed up for the inmate volunteer training program.

During one training session, a guard gave us a tour of the women's jail pod and explained fewer women participated in the ministry sessions than men. She couldn't explain why that was. It seemed odd to me that so few women were interested. And in front of the guard and everyone else on the tour, I said female attendance was going to change. It just popped out of my mouth. Apparently, the weeks I'd spent thinking about this ministry wiped out any of the hesitancy I'd had about participating.

Everyone seemed a little startled by my proclamation. "You watch," I thought to myself, "this program is going to take off." I was convinced the jail ministry needed the right messenger with the right level of enthusiasm and commitment to make it effective. After all, I knew in my heart that I could help the inmates and that they'd be receptive to my message because I truly believed in what I'd be telling them. Besides, the system encouraged them to participate by giving them an incentive—a reduced sentence. That was a pretty good deal. The message as I saw it was, listen to me, learn from me, and you might get out of jail earlier. That was a message I could work with.

The month of training, credentialing, shadowing, and touring went by, and it was time to start the program. Now, I was officially a church jail minister, although the thought of being called a "minister" seemed disingenuous to me. I was proud to be a member of our church and proud to share the Gospel, but to be called a minister felt like a stretch. When I shared this concern at the church, I was told that being a minister simply meant to serve and that I was serving by getting involved in this program. So, "Lauren the Jail Minister" it was.

To prepare for ministering at the jail, I put together a curriculum based on a broadly accepted set of church training programs widely used in similar programs. With the same vigor I put into studying the McDonald's way of doing things and learning the ins and outs of the gas drilling business, I learned this program backward and forward. I knew exactly what topics of discussion, reading assignments, Q&A topics, and recommended prayers I'd be presenting. I was ready. I even brought along a television monitor to share professionally produced videos as part of my presentation. However, as I'd soon learn, even with all the preparation in the world, sometimes the best-laid plans go astray.

On the first Sunday I was scheduled to minister at the Garfield County jail, there were thirteen female inmates. Their crimes varied from drug-related offenses to burglary, domestic violence, and a smattering of other offenses. My office for the day was the jail library, where I set up the video monitor and waited for everyone to come to the meeting. Remember when the guard said female attendance was low? Yeah, that turned out to be true. One inmate showed up. One. I waited and then was told that this inmate was the only one coming—don't expect anyone else. Yeah, well, we'll just have to see about that. I got up, excused myself from the library, and made haste to the jail pod. If they didn't know me before, they did now. I loudly proclaimed that I was a new minister from the church, I had an important message to share with all of them, and I expected them to attend church right now. They looked at me with blank stares. Then I shouted, "Hurry up! Get to the library. We're already late and I have a lot to cover with you. Stop wasting time!" A few minutes later, all thirteen inmates were in the library. They may have looked disgruntled and disinterested, but nevertheless, they were there. Now it was up to me.

I spent the next three hours coming to life as Jail Minister Lauren. Forget the curriculum and the professional videos, I needed to make a personal connection, or I knew I'd lose them before we ever got started. I prayed for them. I asked them questions—hopefully making the process more personal. I took an inspirational approach, and it proved effective. The women were opening up about themselves and participating in a way I don't think any of them had anticipated. While I'd been hopeful, I was encouraged to see everything play out the way I had imagined it.

Boy, did this feel good.

I left the jail feeling I was onto something. Those women were emotionally engaged, and after I shared my own spiritual journey, they even expressed a willingness to live a positive Christian life.

That's life-changing stuff.

For me, connecting with God is a deeply personal and emotional experience. Now these inmates had someone in their life, even if just for a sliver of time every Sunday, who was willing to guide them into their own relationship with God. Given what I'd seen so far, it looked like this new program and new chapter in my life would be successful.

The lessons I gave were a positive take on life, redemption, and restoration—all focused on God's love for us. Each inmate needed to know He's not looking down at you in disappointment. He's not mad at you. In fact, He has a plan for you, one filled with hope and a future—a future filled with good and not evil. All you had to do was reach out and receive His love. I tried to impress upon the inmates that God is for you and not against you, that each of them is a valued person. I believe each of the inmates knew I truly cared about them and their path forward.

For me, success in this mission rested on one fundamental thing— that every person be given an opportunity to reconcile with God. I prayed that each woman would know God forgave her sins, that He knew her shortcomings and failures and loved her anyway. I wanted them to grab hold of the life God intended for them and to understand that walking with Him frees us from the bonds of our past. This was a message they needed to hear, and thankfully, they responded to it.

Empowering incarcerated women was now my passion. It's quite the feeling to help someone embrace faith in God. This is a mission for which I am still passionate. I've made deep connections with people who were otherwise lacking love, support, and faith.

Everything wasn't all rosy, though. Ministering to the jail population wasn't without its frustrations. Many of the inmates were serving relatively short sentences for petty offenses, so I often didn't have the time I needed to make a real impact. Sure, I was glad they were moving on quickly, but I wished I could have helped them more. Others I had such high hopes for relapsed and fell back into their drug habits once they were released. And, sadly, many would be on a never-ending cycle of recidivism. I learned to truly appreciate the victories, no matter how small. A willingness to have a relationship with God, no matter how many challenges someone was facing, was sure to make a positive impact.

For others, the program was an off-the-charts success. A few of the women reached out to me through my church after their release. We found ourselves regularly meeting at the McDonald's with our kids playing together in the PlayPlace, and us talking about God, the church, and the Bible.

Like many counties, Garfield County has a back-to-work program that tries to limit recidivism by helping integrate released inmates back into the workforce. The more quickly someone gets to work, the less likely they are to repeat offenses. Many of the programs incentivize employers to make such hires, subsidizing the wages they'd pay to former convicts. When I later opened my restaurant, I had no interest in taking government money or to, in any way, be perceived as financially benefiting from my participation in the jail ministry program. But I did see how the employment opportunity could help get those in need get back on their feet. Over the years, I made sure Shooters Grill hired some of the released inmates.

On a couple of occasions, we opened our family home to a newly released person. Each of the women had come from difficult circumstances and needed a short-term living arrangement before they could get transitioned. It was the right thing to do, and I felt great to help them at such a time of need.

I spent seven years working in the jail ministry—it's where I learned compassion, patience, perseverance, and how to love the unlovely. These are often people that others dismiss. Some had always been somebody else's problem. I wanted to be a part of their lives and give them hope for a productive and independent life. It meant the world to me.

I often reflect on this time in my life when the political world around me is racing a thousand miles a minute. Who is being forgotten in all of this? Who needs our help the most, and what will our policies as a country do to affect them? I've been there. I've been in the jails. I've worked with those hitting rock bottom. I've seen the compassion of law enforcement firsthand. I've seen the generosity of those in my church. And I've seen the life-changing success that comes with compassion and understanding.

I'm convinced we can change our world for the better by sharing the God-given love in our hearts with everyone, and I'm glad I had a chance to do just that at the Garfield County jail.

When we talk about the need for a hand up to those in need, I mean it because I've seen it. That will always be a better approach than a hand-out. It's tougher to do, but it's worth it.

★ ★ ★

FRENCH FRIES
& FIREARMS

★ ★ ★

CHAPTER 11

Welcome to Shooters Grill

I f you're looking to experience the western way of life, head to Rifle, Colorado.

Rifle is where real cowboys still work. Sometimes you can see one riding his horse along the road when you drive by. It's also the only city I know of in the United States that shares a name with a firearm. The street signs and police cars have the city logo on them that, no surprise, is an image of a rifle.

Rifle is a rural town with about 10,000 residents living near the Colorado River. It's home to cattle ranches, picture-perfect views, and large deposits of clean natural gas that are extracted by the local energy industry.

In 2012, thanks to President Obama and Colorado Democrats who were pushing for highly restrictive energy extraction regulations, the economy was about to go over a cliff. Jayson's contract work for local energy production expired, and we made the tough decision that he go to Texas for the work being offered there. A lot of the local energy workers did the same thing. Jayson would work in a Texas oil patch for two weeks, come back home, and then do it all over again. Rinse and repeat. The uncertainty of his work and distance from home wasn't ideal, but it was necessary—he had a family to support. Though I'd been a stay-at-home mother, I thought it might be a good idea to get a job. We needed the money. I wanted to be productive. Maybe it was time to put some of the food service skills I learned at McDonald's to work?

Around that time, a restaurant called the Cowboy Calf-A closed in downtown Rifle. The landlord was offering a turn-key operation—kitchen equipment, tables, point-of-sales systems, the works. Given the economy, he was a motivated seller and ready to offer attractive terms. Opening a restaurant was an appealing prospect, especially for this girl who'd worked at the McDonald's down the street. Jayson and I talked it over, and even though we saw the building needed plenty of remodeling work, we agreed we could make a go of it.

As anyone who has done it will tell you, opening a restaurant is not for the faint of heart. Even when I went down to start the permitting process, the people in the city's planning department tried to discourage me from doing it. They were coming from a good place and warned me of the challenges, citing how other small businesses in the area were struggling to make ends meet in this down economy.

Here's the thing, though: as you may have seen by now, when someone tells me I can't do something, that's a trigger that makes me work twice as hard to be successful at it. (That would certainly be on display when I decided to run for Congress.) Now I was more determined than ever to move forward, although we had to do it on a tight budget. Jayson and I agreed we'd do a lot of the work ourselves. After the experience we'd had with the mortgage company a few years earlier, we refused to take out a loan to get the restaurant up and running. It was going to be tough, but we convinced ourselves we were up for the task.

Once we committed to moving forward, we got to work, and there was plenty of it. Jayson is never shy about working hard, but this pushed him to the limit. He'd come home from Texas every two weeks and then spend each day and night for his two weeks off remodeling the restaurant. Then the cycle would repeat. With installing the new flooring, the electrical work, remodeling the bathrooms, the painting, and everything else, this was a huge project that wasn't nearly as easy as they make it seem on television remodeling shows.

While Jayson spent his time rehabbing the building, I spent time planning the menu and preparing for the restaurant's launch. I knew from the beginning it would be western-themed and that we needed a solid brand—and a memorable one at that. Then the flash of genius hit. What would be better than naming a restaurant located in the town of Rifle, "Shooters Grill?!" We even named the menu items to reflect our brand. Would you prefer a Guac 9 or a Swiss and Wesson burger? How about the M-16 Burrito or a Ruger Rueben? I added local western decor and American flags. The plan was coming together. Jayson and I were feeling confident that we could open soon. But—

A month into the remodeling effort, we had to hit the brakes. My grandfather in Florida got extremely sick with a C. diff infection. His prognosis wasn't very good, so I flew down immediately to see him. I brought my Roman, who was now eight months old, with me.

My grandfather, who I lovingly called "Papa," was in the hospital, and I stayed by his side every day for two weeks, dressed in the full personal protective gear the hospital required. Papa was listless and struggling. It was awful seeing him suffering so much. I prayed for Papa and reflected on the time I'd spent growing up with him and Granny. They were always there for me, supporting me, encouraging me, and loving me with all they had. As I got older, I often told people Mom was my best friend, and Papa was the dad I never had—a man I was proud of and never wanted to disappoint. As a kid, one of Mom's most effective disciplinary tactics was to threaten to tell Papa when I did something wrong. It worked 100 percent of the time. In fact, it worked so well that Jayson would use it on me too. "You'd better get it together, or I'll tell Papa," he'd say. Guess what? It still worked. Look, I only had one Papa, and I never wanted to let him down.

On my last night at the hospital, Papa was remarkably alert, but based on what the doctors had told me, I knew this was likely the last time I'd ever see him. I brought Roman along, tucked into his car seat, and showed Papa his new great-grandchild from the window of the hospital door. Papa waved and said, "Hello," and Roman laughed and smiled. I entered the room, walked over to Papa's side, removed my glove, and took his hand for the last time. I prayed over him, then kissed him goodbye. This was a devastating time. I didn't know a life without my Papa. As I wrestled with the pain of it all, I left the hospital and drove over to his house. I sat in his workshop and reminisced, taking in the smells and retreating into the memories of my childhood. Papa would be released from the hospital, and he passed away at home.

This was devastating. You should know that from when I was a toddler all the way through high school, I would spend every summer with Papa and Granny, and the lessons they taught me helped make me who I am today.

Granny led by example when it came to earning your way through life. She was a workaholic. Her mother had gone through the Great Depression, so Granny was determined that she would never go without. For decades, she worked at Frito-Lay, and then when she retired from there, she worked for another twenty years at Walmart. When Granny would come home, I'd help her cook dinner, and then at night, we'd all sit around watching television, with me on her lap as she rocked me. She'd sing to me every night despite being the only one in the family with a worse singing voice than me. I loved every minute of it. Granny's favorite hymn was "I'll Fly Away," and it remains my favorite to this day.

Papa was the person I looked up to the most in life. We went fishing almost every day. Whenever he'd get tired, he'd have me hold the fishing pole, and coincidentally, there always happened to be a fish caught on the line. Papa made me feel special and always made time for me. We'd fish, build wood crafts in his shop, work on art projects, and laugh at the silliest of things.

One day, I realized my cousins all had dads, but I didn't. So I asked Papa if he'd be my dad. He told me he loved being my Papa because having a Papa was even better than having just a dad. I adored spending time with him and Granny. Every summer ended on a sad note because I knew it would be a while before I'd see them again. I'd cry for days, knowing how much I'd miss them.

When my own children came along, Granny and Papa treated them just as they'd treated me. This was the pure love I'd learned about as a child, and it was amazing to see my kids experience it as I had. To this day, Granny spends time laughing and telling stories and singing with our family, and the memories of Papa are held dear in all our hearts.

Once I returned to Rifle after Papa passed, I dedicated a section of Shooter's Grill as "Papa's Section." The centerpiece of the newly minted area was a large family table surrounded by framed pictures of Papa, where it gives me joy knowing he's there looking out for everyone.

Granny would come to live with us in Colorado in a small farmhouse on our property that Jayson had renovated. Having her with us means the world to me, and it's allowed the kids to bond with their great-grandmother the same way I did as a kid. Granny reminds us every day why family matters.

Amid all of this, Jayson and I were still working to get Shooters Grill ready to open. By May of that year, we'd done it, and not a moment too soon. Jayson and I were living paycheck to paycheck and needed to get this business generating income. We'd experienced costly delays, and the remodel itself wasn't cheap. But the good news was that Jayson and I were able to manage it all without having to take out a loan.

Once the remodel was complete, we had to finalize the menu and hire staff. We couldn't afford to train the wait staff before we opened, so I asked them to come in early on the morning of opening day, and they got a crash course. The only real rule at the time was that they wear western boots, jeans, and flannel shirts. The rest we'd figure out as we went along.

When we opened the doors, there wasn't a whole lot of fanfare. In fact, there wasn't any. No one in town knew when we were opening, so I went door-to-door in downtown Rifle and invited people to come. I made it easier by offering a free lunch. Even with the free food, it was still less expensive and more effective than the money I would have spent advertising a grand opening. What a great first day! The people who came in left big tips, which all the servers appreciated, and we quickly learned the food was getting rave reviews. Shooters Grill was now open! But with every new venture, all that glitters isn't always gold, and there were a few surprises in store.

When our first payroll came due, the bill from the processing company was much bigger than I'd expected, which led to a lesson about how payroll taxes work. When I called the company to complain that I'd been taxed twice, they explained that payroll taxes are paid on top of the taxes taken from the employee and that I, as the owner, was the one who had to pay them. That's one of the problems with high taxation—it keeps a small business from being able to use that money for things like reinvestment, hiring more staff, or giving raises to the current staff. This was yet another life lesson that would help shape my political thinking. It's not complicated. Lower taxes allow everyone to be more productive. Higher taxes, not so much.

A few weeks after Shooters opened for business came a moment that would change the fortunes of everything—the restaurant's, mine, Jayson's, the staff—forever.

★ ★ ★ CHAPTER 12 ★ ★ ★

The Place Is Packed.
The Waitresses Are Packing.

O ne morning, I walked into the restaurant, and people were abuzz with the big news of the day—a man had been brutally beaten near Shooters and died. When you live in a small place like Rifle, of course, something like this is going to be the talk of the town. My mind raced. What would happen if there was more violence nearby? What if the police don't catch who did this? Were we in danger? I had a restaurant with young female servers. I'm five foot nothing and weigh all of one hundred pounds. I had no way to protect them or myself. How many times had I worked alone at night, closing the restaurant? I thought I'd better do something to protect myself and my staff.

There was a pawn shop across the street from the restaurant, so I walked over and talked with Edward, the guy who owned it. He'd also heard about the beating—I mean, who hadn't? I shared my concerns and expressed interest in buying a gun, but I wasn't sure about the Colorado gun laws. I wondered whether I could obtain a concealed weapons permit. Edward explained that I could open-carry without one. Well, that sure sounded better, quicker, and easier.

I bought a Taurus Judge, a cumbersome five-shot revolver that chambers both a .410 shotgun shell and a .45 Colt cartridge. This was the perfect firearm for me because if I had to use it, a miniature shotshell gave me a better chance of hitting my target without killing an innocent bystander. I didn't want a bullet flying toward an unintended target.

Now that I had a weapon, I bought a holster. I strapped that thing on, slid my Judge into it, and went to work—armed and not defenseless. The customers didn't seem to mind. A few would ask about the gun, mainly about what type it was, then they'd carry on eating. Several even showed me what weapon they were concealing. Yes, you might be surprised to learn just how many people carry concealed guns around every day for personal protection.

To this day, I still use the Judge with .410 shotgun shells as a home defense weapon. I know I can rely on it to hit whatever I'm aiming at. For work, I bought a smaller, semiautomatic Springfield XDS.45, which is much more comfortable and practical to wear. However, to use this one, I needed lessons on how to shoot a semiautomatic weapon.

The presence of my new firearm prompted two of my waitresses to ask if they could carry too. They were persistent, explaining they already had their concealed weapons permits, and while they typically had their guns locked in their cars, they would prefer to open-carry. At first, I was hesitant to let them, but I decided they could open-carry if they'd go target shooting together. That would serve a dual purpose—it would be a good team-building exercise and would help us all become more confident with our weapons. It became a fun routine to head to the gun range after work.

The restaurant was doing well, and one day, a reporter for the local newspaper stopped by to check us out. She was there to learn more about us because Shooters Grill, this new joint, was getting more votes for the Local Choice Awards than the more established restaurants in the nearby town of Glenwood Springs, which was slightly larger than Rifle. Boy, she was in for an eye-opening experience.

Remember, my servers and I openly carried our pistols, on our hips, in holsters. The reporter walked into the restaurant and, noting that it was western-themed, said, "Hey, that's cute that you wear fake guns." To which I replied, "No ma'am, these aren't fake." As you can imagine, that's not the response she was expecting. So, the reporter asked, "Well, the guns aren't loaded, are they?" So, what else would my response be other than, "Of course, they are, ma'am. Why wouldn't they be?" That was it. The story now wasn't about how we carried our food; it was now about how we carried our guns.

That story went viral as soon as it was published.

The next thing I knew, a whole lot more of America was stopping in, not just the regular locals. They wanted to know who were these girls with guns on their hips serving food in Rifle? Lines formed out the door. It was so crazy packed that we had to expand our hours.

ABC News came out with a full crew and featured us on *Nightline,* where correspondent Clayton Sandell noted, "Inside, the place is packed, and the waitresses are packing." Besides the millions who saw the story on television, as of this writing, it's generated more than 4 million views on YouTube. We'd been open barely a year, and I couldn't keep up with the media attention from around the world. Heck, articles were written about Shooters Grill in France, China, Australia, and all corners of the globe. The Shooters Grill Facebook page exploded with tens of thousands of followers. There were no more rush hours; they lasted all day. The shirts we had with the Shooter's logo and emblazoned with "FREEDOM" were consistently sold out.

All of this because one day, I bought a gun for protection.

Just a year before, Jayson and I were trying to figure out how we were going to make this restaurant work, and now, the biggest challenge we had was finding enough help to cover our expanding business.

Shooters was a bona fide success.

My favorite part of the restaurant is the people I meet. And thanks to the publicity we got, I've developed true friendships with people from around the world—a lot of them who made Shooters a must-see part of their travel plans. I've met people on their way to Las Vegas who flew into Denver, rented a car, and drove over the Rocky Mountains to dine with us before continuing to Vegas. Tourists from Japan, Australia, Canada, and all points in between have visited Rifle and eaten at Shooters. It's a unique slice of the American way of life. We proudly display a pin map where everyone who visits marks where they're from.

The locals who stop by the restaurant are some of the best salt-of-the-earth people you'll ever meet, not just in Rifle but anywhere. Among them are my hometown sheriff, Garfield County's Lou Vallario, local law enforcement officers, and plenty of hard-working, God-fearing, freedom-loving Americans. They all know that in my restaurant, they're appreciated.

One of our favorite customers at Shooters is an eighty-something jokester named Ed Chamberlain. Let me tell you, he sure does like to stir the pot with the customers. Ed was born in the nearby town of De Beque and raised in Rifle. He's a lot of things—an Army veteran, a cowboy, and an old-school farmer. Ed refuses to use modern equipment; instead, he prefers workhorses.

Ed has come into Shooters for a cup of coffee almost every day since we've had the doors open. Somehow, he's managed to never pay for a single cup. As Ed explains, he never had to pay for coffee before, so why start now? He tips the waitress, and that's enough for him. Ed makes us laugh with inappropriate jokes and a complete lack of political correctness. He's a sly guy who doesn't know I've caught on to how he purposely talks softly to our servers so that they'll lean in close to hear him. A few years back, a customer took a picture of Ed plowing his field with his horses and brought me a framed copy. To this day, we proudly display it at the restaurant. If you ever see Ed at Shooters, please offer to buy him a cup of coffee. He and I would both appreciate it.

Another of our customers was a gun safety instructor who taught concealed weapons classes. He offered to train our staff, and Jayson and I thought it would be good to open up the class to the general public too. Sixty-five people showed up for the first class, maxing out the capacity of the restaurant. We decided to make this a regular monthly thing. Safety was of paramount importance to us, and we'd shut down the restaurant to hold classes. This sent an important message. Safety first. Americans have the right to gun ownership, but that right also carries with it personal responsibility, which includes treating a weapon with the utmost safety.

Shooters is about so much more than food, and I'm proud of it for so many reasons. Jayson and I overcame plenty of obstacles in launching it. Shooters has helped provide for our family, and it has helped people I care about who needed meaningful work. The restaurant also brought new people to our little town and helped strengthen our sense of community.

It's also the reason I became so interested in our right to bear arms. Shooters inspired me to read the Constitution of the United States of

America. It's why I now know that our rights are God-given and not meant to be dictated to us by distant, power-hungry politicians.

My experiences as a business owner made me think about how the government taxes and regulates businesses and the challenges faced by business owners who assume the responsibility of serving and employing others.

Shooters has taught me very practical day-to-day lessons too. When there's mud on the floor, it reminds me that men and women are out working to produce the natural gas that heats our homes. When the restaurant is busy, I know to roll up my sleeves, hop back in the kitchen, and cook. When payroll is due, I'd better make sure there's enough to pay everybody, including the government. Oh, and the smile that came with my McDonald's uniform still has the same effect on my staff, customers, and me.

Shooters Grill has become much more than just a good steak or burger. It's shown me how many freedom-loving people are proud to associate with those who bring a voice to our shared values. God, country, and guns matter to a lot of people. Owning a place that celebrates and embraces this way of life has made a huge impact that will never be lost on me.

One other thing: back then, if you had told Jayson and me that one day I'd be sitting down and chatting with the President of the United States of America about our little restaurant, where the waitresses have real guns on their hips and you can "Trump" your burger, we never would have believed you.

But in America, anything is possible.

CHAPTER 13

Pretty Little Mugshots

The number of people who came into Shooters Grill every day continued to grow. Due in no small part to the incredible press we'd gotten, the seats were filled—some people came for the comradery, some for the pretty gals wearing guns on their thighs, and everyone came back for another really good burger. Regardless of the reasons, Shooters was firing on all cylinders, and we now had a chance to be a food vendor for one of the biggest entertainment events in Colorado.

Country Jam is an annual summer music festival in Mack, Colorado, which draws some of the biggest stars in country music and tens of thousands of fans over a four-day weekend. It generates more than $10 million a year for the local economy, and for a vendor, it can mean big business. In 2015, Shooters was one of those vendors.

There, on the Western Slope, fun-loving people from every walk of life eat, drink, and camp in an old hayfield and share their love of country music. They arrive in quarter-million-dollar recreational vehicles or beat-up trucks that can barely start. And for those four days, you'll meet business owners, city councilmen, or young people who barely scraped together the money to buy a ticket. Come June, Country Jam is the place to be.

The layout is a big main stage with hundreds of VIP seats directly below and a field of open seating just beyond. The field is surrounded by smaller stages for lower-level acts, huge catering tents, hundreds of por-ta-potties, and vendor booths toward the back. There's a carnival atmo-sphere with vendors hawking everything from tattoos to fried turkey legs. The music plays all day and into the night.

The Mesa County Sheriff's Office sets up its own operation on site. And the local news media issues daily Country Jam incident reports with the number of arrests for disorderly conduct, minors in possession, and other infractions you'd expect when thousands of people come together and drink all day. Most people around here know someone who, at some point in their life, has been arrested at Country Jam. In that environ-ment, stuff happens that usually makes for an entertaining story down the road.

With Shooters as a vendor, one of my bigger challenges was keeping our young employees focused on work. As you'd expect, there are a lot of distractions at Country Jam, and for my staff, that included hunky cow-boys who'd catch their eye. On the third day of the festival, a Saturday, I noticed one of my employees had been on a break longer than I expected her to be, so I left the Shooters booth to look for her.

As I made my way through the crowd, I found myself near the sher-iff's detention area, where a young woman was sitting in a chair hold-ing a citation and asking a sheriff's deputy if she could leave. She was pointing and explaining that her mother was nearby. It seemed odd the deputy wasn't allowing the gal to leave. I mean, she'd already been given a citation. The longer the deputy kept her there, the more upset the young woman got. Then, as she began to stand up, the deputy aggressively grabbed her and sat her back down. I couldn't believe what I was seeing.

Without hesitation, I started yelling from about fifteen yards away and quickly made my way over. I was fired up. It bothered me seeing this young gal being treated so harshly. I had a lot of questions for the deputy—Is she under arrest? Is she being detained? Have you read her rights to her?

The deputy wasn't interested in what I had to say. He told me this was none of my concern and that I was interfering. The deputy ordered me to leave. I refused. Instead, I told the woman she had rights and that the deputy either needed to arrest her or release her. During this, another deputy showed up, yet I refused to back down. As far as I was concerned, the first deputy had overstepped his bounds when he aggressively forced this gal back into a chair and tried to intimidate her. Someone needed to have her back, and that someone was going to be me—regardless of the cost.

By now, it was a cacophony of yelling between me and the two deputies. They were ordering me to leave, and as they did, I brought out my smartphone and began recording them on video. I threatened to show it to the news media, and that's when one of them threatened me with arrest if I didn't stop. I had every right to be there and told him so. I felt I hadn't done anything wrong. A deputy then tried grabbing the phone out of my hand, and the next thing I knew, I was in handcuffs and on my way to the detention area.

After twenty minutes of sitting there alone and handcuffed, I was handed a citation for disorderly conduct. A deputy took me through processing, cut off my Country Jam wristband, escorted me outside gates, and told me to leave.

And that's what I got for trying to help someone.

The entire episode was upsetting on so many fronts—a young woman had been mistreated, I had to leave my business, and I was going to miss Tim McGraw headline that night. What didn't upset me was my detainment or the citation. I was proud to have stood up for that woman. And for the record, I have the utmost respect for law enforcement. I've made many friends in the law enforcement community, but I wouldn't hesitate to call out a friend for misbehaving, and with that young woman, I believe the deputies misbehaved. As far as how I was treated, I have no hard feelings—those deputies were just doing their job in trying to deescalate a tense situation.

The woman would be released. Mission accomplished. It was time to move on, although life doesn't always work out that way. I made the mistake of missing my court date. When I later went down to settle the matter, I signed paperwork I hoped would resolve everything—this meant I'd be getting a mugshot and meeting with a deputy district attorney. We sat down, I explained what happened, and he told me the case was dismissed.

Later, I was told the entire incident should be expunged from my record, and thankfully, that would mean the mugshot would be expunged too. But, as I've said, life doesn't always work out exactly the way we want it to, and I ended up getting another mugshot to go along with the first one.

About a year later, in July 2016, my life was beyond hectic. Shooters Grill was humming along, and we'd expanded into catering and other food concepts. I worked long hours, sometimes eighteen to twenty hours a day, cooking, filling in for staff who called in sick, promoting the business, and trying to balance all of that with our home life—where Jayson's energy work meant an "on-again, off-again" travel schedule every couple of weeks.

This was all happening at the same time we were remodeling a restaurant across the street from Shooters. It had gone out of business, so Jayson and I decided we'd expand Shooters into that space. I literally had no free time.

One night, Jayson and I closed up Shooters at 10:30 and left for home, which meant heading up Stephens Hill, the steepest and most dangerous road in town. It's a tough drive during the day, but especially so at night. There's a tight hairpin turn with no guardrail where plenty of people have had accidents; some have even died.

With that in mind, I drove slowly up the hill, but danger was literally around the corner as my front wheel caught the edge of the shoulder, and the truck slid off the side and flipped into a ditch fifteen feet below.

Jayson and I were upside down in the truck. The two of us climbed from the truck and surveyed the damage. I tried calling 911 to report the accident, but up there on Stephens Hill, we couldn't get any cell service. Our house was about a mile away, so Jayson and I decided to walk home. The second we got into cell range, I again called the police department, and the dispatcher told me a state patrol officer had already arrived at the scene of our accident.

The dispatcher and I agreed it would be quicker for Jayson and me to go home, get our other truck, and drive back to meet up with the trooper, which we did. When we arrived, we told the trooper what had happened. And while he felt bad, he still wrote me a ticket for careless driving. Jayson and I tied a rope to our wrecked truck, tied the other end to our other truck, and pulled it from the ditch as the trooper watched. Then we towed it home.

Outside of that accident, not a lot changed for the next several months. We were still busy with Shooters, the expansion, the remodeling, and Jayson's hectic work schedule. One particular morning the following February summed up what our harried life had become. After having worked all night, I put on a pair of sweatpants and packed the kids into the car to take them all to school. I was exhausted and looked it. I hadn't showered or brushed my hair, and let's just say I wasn't looking my best.

On that day, I had a lot of things on the to-do list that needed to get done, including a big catering order that I had to deliver to the airport in a few hours. I was in such a hurry that I didn't even notice the patrol lights from a police car flashing behind me. Yep, I was being pulled over for speeding. I wasn't that worried about it—I'd already dropped off two of the kids at school, and even with this delay, I'd still be able to drop off Kaydon and make it back to the restaurant in time to meet the catering delivery deadline. I sent the cook at the restaurant a quick text message to let him know what was going on while I waited for the officer. As I sat in the front seat with the officer in my rear-view mirror, it seemed he was taking longer than usual to approach my window. Then I saw a second officer arrive.

Uh-oh. This can't be good, I thought.

So, I sent the cook another text telling him to move ahead without me because clearly something was happening here.

The officers walked up together to my vehicle, but I knew both of them, so how bad could this be? Whenever you ask, "How bad could this be," it's almost always bad. The officers asked me to get out of the car—turns out, there was a warrant for my arrest because I'd failed to pay a ticket. My mind was racing. I thought back to the wreck on Stephens Hill. Did I pay the ticket I got that night? I thought I had.

Nope, I had not.

Since I was somewhat known around town because of the publicity Shooters Grill had gotten about our open-carry policy, the officers asked if I had any guns on me or in my truck. I told them I didn't, that I was just trying to get my kids to school.

The officers handled the situation professionally, politely, and with as much grace as possible. They even called Jayson for me, so he could come pick up Kaydon. Then they drove me to the police station, where I was taken through the booking process.

Unfortunately, I knew from my previous experience what was coming my way. This wasn't going to be good at all. I also knew another mugshot was in my future, and messy hair and a hoodie don't make for a great look.

By now, Jayson, Kaydon, and my youngest son had arrived at the station. They could see me, and the boys were smiling and waving, excited to see me. They were enjoying watching the scene play out with far too much enthusiasm for my taste. I could only imagine how often I would hear about this. "Hey, mom, remember when you got arrested taking me to school that one morning?"

This was not a proud mom moment.

It took about fifteen minutes to be processed. Then I paid the one-hundred-dollar fine and was released.

So, a lot has been made of my mugshots, but now you know the story.

Is my life hectic? Yes. Did I simply forget to follow up? Did I somehow convince myself that I didn't do anything wrong? Maybe. But when it gets down to it, I don't really have an excuse. I should have shown up to court. I should have paid the tickets on time. I should have shown law enforcement the respect they deserved. I should have played by the rules.

That said, what really amounted to some minor issues (a dismissed disorderly conduct citation and forgetting to pay a ticket for a self-reported traffic accident) would escalate years later in a very big way.

Democrats, as they do, would work double-time to convince the world I was a lawless, dangerous criminal. They'd spend millions of dollars plastering my mugshots across all forms of media, going so far as to slap "WANTED" across the mugshots.

Welcome to politics.

But that was still a couple of years away. For the moment, I had a restaurant to run and more lessons to learn.

Politics was right around the corner.

A GUN-THEMED RESTAURANT OWNER BECOMES A GUN RIGHTS ADVOCATE

CHAPTER 14

Gathering Signatures and Steam

If you want a quick snapshot of what ordinary hard-working Americans are thinking about their government, spend a morning sipping coffee and eating breakfast at Shooters Grill. This isn't a politically correct atmosphere. Our entire restaurant has a vibe that says, "Free speech is alive and welcomed, so please speak your mind!"

We encourage our customers to talk about freedom, politics, and religion. Open dialogue and the sharing of ideas is a healthy thing that should happen more in our society.

One day, in March 2019, a day like any other, the customers were fired up about the National Popular Vote Compact, or SB 19-042, just signed by Colorado governor, Jared Polis. As it read, it was an act "concerning adoption of an agreement among the states to elect the President of the United States by national popular vote."

This was an obvious scheme cooked up by the liberals in Denver to steal our votes for President and an overt attempt to circumvent the

United States Constitution, displace a state's Electoral College votes, and instead elect the Presidential candidate who won the popular vote. This was clearly a knee-jerk reaction to the fact that Hillary Clinton had defeated President Trump in the popular vote but lost in the Electoral College.

The Electoral College system was created so that people in all fifty states would have equal representation when it came to electing a President. Otherwise, today, heavily populated cities like Los Angeles, New York City, Chicago, and Boston would, in effect, elect the President. Given that each of those cities is heavily blue, the Electoral College protects the rest of America from having its President chosen by one group of people. If Democrats got their way, the United States would never be able to elect another Republican President, likely ever.

For those of us who believe in the Constitution, the National Popular Vote Compact (NPV) was a blatant attempt to thwart the election rules laid out in the Constitution so a few Democratic states could steal the presidency. But back in March, I didn't know any of this. I was just a restaurant owner. I'd never heard of the NPV, let alone done anything about it. That changed thanks to my customers at Shooters Grill.

They really piqued my curiosity, so I started researching the NPV. I came across a Facebook page talking about an effort to repeal it led by then-Mesa County Commissioner Rose Pugliese. I decided to get involved and messaged the group, asking how I could help. Soon after, a local volunteer stopped by with signature packets and a nifty badge. She spent time giving me the ins and outs of volunteering and how to maintain the integrity of the signatures. I was shown how to keep secure possession of the petitions and how to verify the signatures I'd gathered were valid. Too bad liberal states didn't do the same thing for the 2020 Presidential election. But that's another story.

The volunteer coordinator handed me ten packets, each of which had forty signature lines. So, to do the math, I needed to gather 400 signatures to do my part. By the third day, I needed more packets. Evidently, a whole lot of Coloradans felt just like I did about the NPV. I'd never done anything like this before, and it felt good to contribute. The people I spoke with seemed genuinely appreciative of my effort and were glad to sign the petitions once I explained what was going on.

As with the jail ministry in Garfield County, a fearless evangelist mentality kicked in. With what little free time I had, I gathered signatures from one end of town to the other—I approached strangers in the supermarket, people walking downtown, and recruited businesses to join the cause. I even traveled to nearby towns. Heck, I turned into a community organizer without realizing it.

Since I had experience dealing with the media with the publicity from Shooters Grill, I put it to good use trying to gin up coverage about our petition efforts. A television station from Denver sent a news crew out to Rifle, which turned into a big media event. Members of "Boots on the Ground Bikers for Trump" led a flag-waving effort along one of our streets. Cars honked up and down every block, and most importantly, scores of people signed the petitions. The news crew interviewed a lot of people frustrated with Denver liberals trying to steal our votes.

The news producer applauded our efforts and seemed to share our enthusiasm for the story. He promised he'd stay in touch and let me know when the story would air. But after a few days, I saw for the first time how liberals can not only control a narrative but will engage in censorship to do so. The story hadn't yet aired, and I hadn't heard back from the producer, so I called him. He told me his boss killed the story and that it was never going to air. No reason was given as to why the story was killed, but I think we all know why. No liberal-controlled media outlet was about to run a story about a bunch of open-carrying, motor-cycle-riding rednecks from western Colorado trying to stop Denver's mighty Democrat machine.

Once again, out of necessity, I needed to find another way to accomplish something. This time, I turned to United States Representative Scott Tipton, the Republican congressman for my district. He'd stopped by Shooters Grill a while back for a meet and greet with the customers. Though I was very appreciative he'd stopped by, my impression of Tipton was he seemed too soft-spoken and lacked a fire in his belly. Nevertheless, he was the first member of Congress I'd ever met, and I figured he must know what he's doing. A congressman surely could be a big help with the petition drive and would help amplify the need for action on repealing NPV.

I called Tipton's office, explained the situation to one of his staffers, and asked if the congressman would issue a statement or attend a signature-gathering event. Colorado's vote for the President of the United States was on the line, and that was an important cause to support. The staffer explained that NPV was a state issue, not a federal one, and said Tipton wouldn't be getting involved. Still, I wasn't deterred and pointed out the Presidency is very much a federal issue and that we didn't have a big ask. All we wanted was for Tipton to encourage more people to sign the petition and reassure the volunteers their efforts weren't in vain. The staffer said, "Sorry, Congressman Tipton is focusing on the 2020 election."

That rejection made me think—hmmm, maybe I should focus on the 2020 election. Now that I'm sitting in Tipton's old chair in the House of Representatives, I'll bet that staffer now wishes he hadn't disregarded me.

In any case, I doubled down and was even more driven. I gathered more and more and more signatures—the momentum was like a runaway locomotive. This was an important cause, and I just couldn't let it go. Who did the Denver liberals think they were to try and take away our state's Electoral College vote?

Before this petition signature drive began, my entire life was Jayson, my boys, home, church, and Shooters Grill. Now it included a burgeoning interest in the political process—talking to a broader group of people, in and around my community, Colorado, and online. Along the way, I discovered there were more people than I'd imagined who shared the same concerns and frustration about what liberals were trying to do to America. I was happy to be a part of the solution and to encourage others to do the same.

After what seemed a never-ending effort, the deadline to turn in those signatures arrived. Commissioner Pugliese held an NPV repeal event in Grand Junction and invited me to attend. Pugliese made the announcement that we'd collected enough signatures needed to put the repeal issue on the November ballot. This would be the first time in Colorado since 1932 that a citizen-led effort to repeal a state law would make it on the ballot. In all, we'd collected more than 228,000 signatures.

Everyone in that room felt a real sense of accomplishment. We'd all worked together and succeeded in doing something historic. I was just proud to be part of the effort, but out of the blue came something I'd not expected. Pugliese got on the mic, called me out of the crowd, and announced that I'd collected the second-highest number of signatures in the entire state. I knew I'd collected quite a few but had no idea it was that many! People applauded the accomplishment. Boy, did I feel good. This sort of political involvement was all new to me, but I already felt empowered.

Seems there was no stopping me now. After the NPV repeal event, I was invited to be on a podcast to talk about the Second Amendment,

Shooters Grill, and the NPV repeal effort. My first podcast interview! The host was nice, very much so, and thought the interview went so well that he arranged for me to speak at an upcoming Lincoln Day Dinner. I was so excited that I agreed to do it before I even knew what a Lincoln Day Dinner was!

The dinner was in Washington state, and as I'd find out, this was a big deal. Dinesh D'Souza was the featured speaker. The local Republican party flew Jayson and me up there and scheduled me to speak for about ten minutes before Dinesh. If you don't know who he is, Dinesh D'Souza is a *New York Times* bestselling author and conservative filmmaker—a huge voice in the conservative movement.

At the time, I didn't know who he was. Remember, before the NPV repeal issue, I was basically just a restaurant owner and mother. As I prepared for this speaking engagement, I became aware that Dinesh was a big deal, so I read one of his books. Then another. Then another. They were incredible! Both he and his lovely wife, Debbie, had lived under socialistic regimes and had a unique perspective on what it's like to live in America versus anywhere else in the world. I now saw there was no Chinese or Russian or Cuban dream, just the American Dream. Even the poorest among us have it better than most anywhere else in the world. We see it every day at our southern border. People are desperately trying to live in our country. If it was better in their country than in America, they wouldn't try so hard to get in. Dinesh loves America and values its freedoms, but he had a warning for us—while the American Dream is alive, we've become complacent, and freedom is fragile.

I read his books and thought, "Go, Dinesh!" I was officially a fan.

Jayson and I flew up to Washington, and though this sort of thing was new to me, I still felt fairly comfortable knowing I only had to speak for ten minutes. My plan was to talk about the Second Amendment and how Denver's liberals were hacking away at our gun rights—plus, I'd talk about how the Democrats were trying to steal our votes for President and my involvement in the effort to stop them. I'd never spoken in public before—well, not at something like this anyway—so I practiced my speech in front of the mirror.

When Jayson and I walked in, I was stunned to see such a huge ballroom, and I learned 600 people were expected. Six hundred. That was the same number of students enrolled in all of Rifle High School at the time. For this small-town girl, to say I was nervous would be an understatement. Before the dinner, Jayson and I were invited to a round-table conversation with members of the local GOP, community leaders, elected officials, and big-dollar party donors. We'd chat about the issues of the day, and Dinesh would give us a ten-minute preview of his speech.

Great!

The event was a formal affair—not black tie but certainly a suit and tie for guys and a nice dress for the ladies. Jayson and I are from a small, rural town. We had no idea what to wear. I showed up in a Shooters Grill t-shirt and jeans. Jayson wore a nice shirt, and he, too, was wearing jeans. We felt awkward at our table, and not just because of how we were dressed. The more people spoke, the more insecure I felt. These were well-educated people. Why would they want to listen to anything I had to say?

As we eased into the evening, I began to relax and enjoy the discussion. Just as I started to feel comfortable, the event organizer walked over and asked if I'd cover for Dinesh since he was running behind. I was a guest, so I felt obligated to say "Yes." What was I to do?! My heart was now about to jump out of my body. It was beating so fast. If I was insecure before, how do you think I felt now? I was a restaurant owner from

Rifle, not a *New York Times* bestselling author. I nodded "Yes" while my mind screamed "No!"

For the briefest of moments, Dinesh was no longer my new hero. Then he showed up. Dinesh gave us that ten-minute preview of his speech and immediately went back on my "good guy" list.

After Dinesh's chat at the table, I was caught off guard when the host thanked him and then invited me to go up and say "Hello." So, there I was in front of this crowd of A-list, educated conservatives, and on-the-fly, I decided to talk about some of the problems with school curriculums and how important it is for conservatives to get involved with local school board elections. For us in Colorado, that meant trying to stop a progressive sex-education curriculum, one that starts in the third grade and teaches gender identity and same-sex issues.

The group was very kind and supportive and left me feeling more confident about the upcoming main event.

When it was time to speak in front of that crowd of 600, I opened by telling them what had happened earlier with my impromptu talk. They were in stitches when I said public speaking made me so nervous that all the saliva from my mouth rushed to my armpits instead. I made it through the speech, and overall, I'd done okay. Many of the same people who'd intimidated me just hours earlier were now showering me with praise. Dinesh would even give me a shout-out on Twitter later that night.

This had all been such a whirlwind, and yet, I had not only survived but thrived. I knew more than ever that I had a voice and that maybe I could make more of a difference than I'd ever thought possible. Something in me was building steam, but I wasn't quite sure what it was.

Unknown to me at the time, I'd soon be face-to-face with a man named Robert Francis O'Rourke, and everything would start coming together.

★ ★ ★ CHAPTER 15 ★ ★ ★

"Hell no, Beto."

I n 2018, Beto O'Rourke was a big deal. He was the shiny show pony for Democrats hoping to turn Texas blue. O'Rourke was running for United States Senate against the Republican incumbent, Senator Ted Cruz, and the mainstream media and the national Democrat party— pretty much the same thing—were all in on the faux Latino from El Paso. Money poured into his campaign coffers, and the energetic cult of personality turned him into a celebrity.

Because most of the national news media acts as the propaganda arm of the Democratic National Committee, O'Rourke's grassroots campaign gained so much traction that he had huge crowds at his rallies, and somehow, people were convinced he could defeat Cruz. And if he didn't, O'Rourke would still be established on the national stage as a potential Presidential candidate who Democrats hoped could defeat President Donald Trump.

The Left bought into their self-created hype, big time. O'Rourke also wasn't known as Beto O'Rourke. He was simply Beto. "Beto is good looking!" "Beto cares about people!" "Beto is cool!" He was Barack

Obama, John F. Kennedy, and Bill Clinton playing saxophone on the *Arsenio Hall Show* all rolled into one.

The message caught traction, the crowds grew, the media hype accelerated, the polls tightened, and money flowed. O'Rourke raised a then-record $80 million for his Senate race and spent almost every dime of it to build his liberal hipster brand, which included gun control and being open to abolishing the United States Immigration and Customs Enforcement Agency (ICE).

The contrast in the race was clear. Cruz ran as the staunch Constitutional conservative he is with the policy positions to match—secure borders, support for ICE, family values, pro-life, lower taxes, and a strong military.

November 2018 came. And despite spending those tens of millions of dollars, O'Rourke lost, and Cruz was reelected. Nevertheless, there was a silver lining for the wannabe political superstar—the results of the race were closer than one might have expected in red Texas, so as far as the Democrats were concerned, their new star was born.

Suddenly, the United States representative from El Paso and now failed Senate candidate was a viable candidate to take on President Trump for the presidency. I was back at home in Rifle, running my restaurant and not paying particularly close attention to all the hype, but even I was like, "Beto O'Rourke? Really?"

That way of thinking would change soon enough.

The following spring, O'Rourke hit the Presidential campaign trail, and all of America was learning more about this amazing man now blessing us with his presence. We learned of his coolness and how he skateboarded and played bass in a post-hardcore rock band. Beto, as the cool kids knew him, graced the cover of *Vanity Fair*, and the media did its level-best, anointing him as their savior.

The problem in all this was O'Rourke himself—he was his own worst enemy, a greenhorn in this new world of national politics. One day he'd say something flippant, like how his wife raised their three children, "sometimes with my help,"[2] then apologize when it blew up in his face. He told the reporter from *Vanity Fair* how he was "born" to be in the Presidential race. Gaffes for sure, but not deal-breakers.

O'Rourke's background surely went against the "every man" myth he tried cultivating. He attended boarding schools, had an Ivy League education, married a billionaire's daughter, and had a self-reported worth of $9 million. What did he do to earn any of that? Yet here he was railing against white "privilege." That's what real progressives do, even though he's white himself. So, essentially, O'Rourke was railing against—himself.

At the time, if you'd have asked the average person, they'd have told you Beto O'Rourke was a Hispanic. After all, he's from El Paso, a city that, according to the United States Census Bureau, is nearly 83 percent Hispanic. And since "Beto" is a common Latino nickname for "Roberto," surely he's Hispanic, people thought. Not even close.

The entire image he presented was a mirage, a purely political contrivance.

"Beto" was born Robert Francis O'Rourke—a white Irish American whose father was an El Paso County commissioner and then an El Paso County judge. O'Rourke's father, Pat O'Rourke, understood local Texas politics and dreamed of such a future for his son. He didn't believe the primarily Mexican American voting bloc in El Paso would embrace a white Irishman named Robert. So he threw his real family heritage under the bus, and "Beto" was born.

---

[2] Matt Visor. March 14, 2019. 8:12 a.m. https://twitter.com/mviser/status/1106181227386732545

According to the *Dallas Morning News*,[3] Pat explained why he gave Robert the nickname, "Nicknames are common in Mexico and along the border, and if he ever ran for office in El Paso, the odds of being elected in this mostly Mexican-American city were far greater with a name like Beto than Robert Francis O'Rourke."

So it was all a con—sort of like the time Hillary Clinton spoke in a fake southern accent on a campaign trip down south. It's a page ripped from the DNC playbook, which they've used with great success and likely always will. Consider how Sandy Cortez, a girl who grew up in the affluent neighborhood of Yorktown Heights, New York, turned herself into the virtue-signaling, wildly popular paragon of progressivism and wannabe socialist congresswoman we now know as Alexandria Ocasio-Cortez.

This tactic feels icky, gross, and manipulative because that's exactly what it is.

A big part of O'Rourke's appeal wasn't just his name and contrived Hispanic heritage. His policy positions were also a liberal wish list of anti-Constitutional platitudes, like gun control. He'd always strongly advocated for it, but during a Democratic Presidential primary debate on September 12, 2019, Robert Francis made it clear he didn't want to *control* guns; he wanted to *confiscate* them.[4]

Moderator David Muir: "Some on this stage have suggested a voluntary buy-back for guns in this country. You've gone further. You've said, quote, 'Americans who own AR-15s and AK-47s

---

3   Corchado, Alfredo. "Beto O'Rourke's El Paso roots may be key in his uphill battle against Ted Cruz." *Dallas Morning News* March 10, 2018

4   ABC News. "Read the full transcript of ABC News' 3rd Democratic debate." September 13, 2019 https://abcnews.go.com/US/read-full-transcript-abc-news-3rd-democratic-debate/story?id=65587810

will have to sell them to the government, all of them.' You know that critics call this confiscation. Are you proposing taking away their guns? And how would this work?"

O'Rourke: "I am, if it's a weapon that was designed to kill people on a battlefield. If the high-impact, high-velocity round, when it hits your body, shreds everything inside of your body, because it was designed to do that, so that you would bleed to death on a battlefield and not be able to get up and kill one of our soldiers. When we see that being used against children, and in Odessa, I met the mother of a 15-year-old girl who was shot by an AR-15, and that mother watched her bleed to death over the course of an hour because so many other people were shot by that AR-15 in Odessa and Midland, there weren't enough ambulances to get to them in time. Hell, yes, we're going to take your AR-15, your AK-47. We're not going to allow it to be used against our fellow Americans anymore."

For the record, I don't believe guns cause violence. I believe it is the evil in man that illegally shoots and kills. It is our right to ably defend ourselves from such evil.

O'Rourke followed up his debate performance with a post on Twitter, "Hell yeah, we're going to take your AR-15. If it's a weapon that was designed to kill people on the battlefield, we're going to buy it back." [5]

By the way, an AR-15 isn't used on the battlefield.

O'Rourke would make the media rounds in the days that followed, and when pressed, he repeated his desire for gun confiscation. When asked by CNN's Chris Cuomo, "Are you, in fact, in favor of gun

---

[5] Beto O'Rourke. September 12, 2019. 8:26 p.m. https://twitter.com/Beto ORourke/status/1172320706526269440

confiscation?" O'Rourke answered, "Yes, when it comes to AR-15's and AK-47's designed for military use on the battlefield... So, when it comes to those weapons, Chris, the answer is yes."[6]

With CNN's Alisyn Camerota, he tried backpedaling by calling confiscation "a mandatory buyback."[7] But it was with MSNBC's Joe Scarborough where O'Rourke's answer to what he would do if people refused to sell back their guns looked like it was ripped from the pages of *Mein Kampf*, "Just as in any law that is not followed or flagrantly abused, there have to be consequences or else there is no respect for the law. So, in that case, I think there would be a visit by law enforcement to recover that firearm and to make sure that it is purchased, bought back, so that it cannot be potentially used against somebody else."[8]

Wow! O'Rourke planned to send armed officers to your home to take your guns. That should have scared the heck out of any freedom-loving American.

O'Rourke's denials of gun confiscation couldn't even get past the left-leaning PolitiFact, a non-profit fact-checker, which claims to be nonpartisan. They analyzed his debate and media exchanges and concluded, "We rate O'Rourke's claim that he is 'not talking about confiscating anybody's guns' as False."[9]

And so there it was, finally out in the open for all to see. The darling of the Democrats and potential leader of the free world wanted to confiscate legal firearms from American citizens. Sure, President Obama

---

[6] *Cuomo Prime Time*. CNN. September 18, 2019. http://edition.cnn.com/TRANSCRIPTS/1909/18/CPT.01.html

[7] *New Day*. CNN. October 16, 2019. https://transcripts.cnn.com/show/nday/date/2019-10-16/segment/06

[8] *Morning Joe*. MSNBC. October 14, 2019. https://youtu.be/FKPD98NmRuE

[9] Kertscher, Tom. "Presidential candidate Beto O'Rourke falsely claims he hasn't talked about confiscating guns." PolitiFact, October 21, 2019

told us we were clinging to our guns. But he also told us he wasn't going to take them, so who were we to believe?

Nine other Democrat Presidential candidates on the debate stage failed to counter O'Rourke. So, the only conclusion for me was that O'Rourke had said what the pro-Second Amendment crowd had always claimed to be true and what the Democrats and mainstream media had always tried to deny. This was indeed a smoking gun.

I was pissed. I was a gun owner—a proud gun owner. We were always being told to stay calm, that it was crazy to believe anyone would come take our guns. I couldn't believe nobody seemed to be sticking up for us and saying what needed to be said.

But as good fortune would have it, I saw O'Rourke was planning to speak in Colorado the day after telling CNN he'd confiscate our guns. He had a rally scheduled in Aurora, the perfect place for him to peddle his anti-gun message. You may recall Aurora was where, in 2012, a mass murderer named James Holmes unleashed pure evil by opening fire in a movie theater. He killed twelve defenseless people and injured seventy others.

Colorado already had the momentum O'Rourke was looking for. Just months before it passed a restrictive Red Flag gun seizure law. Gun rights in the state were under attack.

I lived in Aurora as a kid, and now some tyrannical candidate was headed there to tell me I shouldn't have the right to defend myself with a gun. This guy would make us less safe. Evil exists in this world, and you can't defend against it with rainbows and unicorns. O'Rourke would do what a lot of liberal candidates do: he'd use Colorado's defenseless victims, who no longer had a voice of their own, to bolster his own mission to take our guns away.

I decided to tell him how I felt.

So, one week to the day after that Presidential primary debate, I woke up, got dressed, put my Glock on my hip, and drove three hours to Aurora City Hall. I almost always open-carry my handgun, and that day would be no exception. On the drive up, my mind was racing. At that time, I didn't do politics. I didn't go to Presidential rallies. I thought, What could I possibly accomplish by going to this one? I was filled with a strange mix of determination, fear of the unknown, and being ticked off. The good thing was it made the drive fly by—or I may have been speeding.

When I arrived at City Hall, there were hundreds of rally attendees and press. Dozens of women from "Moms Demand Action," a gun-control group, were gathered nearby. I thought, "I'm a mom, I'm demanding action, but they sure don't speak for me. How dare they co-opt my motherhood for their cause." I decided to go to the opposite end of where they were.

I quickly realized people noticed I was packing and didn't want me there. I heard their comments. They didn't want to just take away my gun rights. They wanted to shut me up.

Meanwhile, O'Rourke was running an hour behind schedule. So, while I waited, this quickly turned into the worst experience ever— worse than waiting in the doctor's office lobby and worse than having your mugshot plastered all over town. More on that later.

There was a woman standing next to me who was doing a Facebook Live who pointed her smartphone at me, making sure her audience of ten could see my gun. She was just appalled, she said, that a "gun nut" had shown up. A guy behind me agreed. So I replied to both, "Yeah, hello. I'm standing right here. I can hear you. But since you brought it up, I have every right to be here to defend my right to own a firearm."

Talk about awkward.

At that moment, a reporter saw the gun holstered on my hip and asked why I was there. He told me that if I got the chance to ask O'Rourke a question, he'd like to talk with me after. That struck me as odd since I didn't know you could ask a question at a rally.

Up near the steps, I noticed a woman who appeared to be a campaign staffer holding a microphone. I made my way over and asked her if there'd be an opportunity to ask a question. She said there would be, so I asked if I could ask one. She said yes. Uh-oh. Anxiety set in. I had no idea what I should say. Public speaking is supposed to be one of the most nerve-racking experiences a person can have, and my nerves were racked there on the steps of Aurora's city hall. I looked up and saw security detail everywhere. Snipers. Armed police. Oh, the irony.

O'Rourke finally showed up to a bunch of cheers. I was somewhat disappointed he didn't ride his skateboard in. I was more disappointed when he spent most of his time bashing President Trump. But mainly, I was growing more flat-out scared as the minutes passed. I was nearing my self-inflicted crunch time.

The microphone lady must have had a second, closer look at me and my sidearm because she came over to confirm that I was going to be respectful. I reassured her I would be. Someone handed me a microphone, and it was "go time." It's been said bravery is being scared but still doing whatever it is that scares you. Time to find out just how brave I was.

I'd like to tell you that this was rehearsed. I'd like to tell you I knew what I'd say. I'd like to tell you I remembered what I was saying. But the reality is that it was all a blur. I couldn't even hear myself talking, but the video transcript revealed that I came through and shared my concerns pretty well.[10]

---

[10] "RAW: Beto O'Rourke holds town hall meeting in Aurora" 9News. KUSA-TV. September 19, 2019. https://youtu.be/tNXe6eHFhBo

I stood at the front of the crowd as O'Rourke looked down at me, steps away from where I was standing. I began to speak. That was my voice I heard over the microphone. Here goes nothing!

Me: Hello, thank you so much for taking my question. My name is Lauren Boebert and I drove down here from Rifle, Colorado to speak with you today. I was one of the gun-owning Americans that heard your speech and heard what you had to say regarding 'hell yes, we're going to take your AR-15s and your AK-47s…

(Crowd interrupts with jeers.)

O'Rourke: Let's be respectful. Let's be respectful.

Me: Well, I am here to say, hell no, you're not.

(Crowd jeers loudly.)

Me: So with that, I would like to know how you intend to legislate evil. Because it is not the gun, it is the heart of the man that does that. We all have stories…

(Crowd grows louder with disagreement.)

Me: Excuse me.

O'Rourke: Let's, let's allow her to finish, please, please, please.

Me: Thank you. We all have these stories; we all have the experiences. I was living in Aurora during Columbine. I had just recently moved, um, when the Aurora shootings happened, yet I have very close ties here, yet all of those people were there defenseless. They had no way to defend themselves against a crazed shooter, so I want to know how you intend to legislate the hearts of men and leave American citizens like my, like myself. American mothers, I have four children, I'm five foot zero one-hundred pounds, cannot really defend myself with a fist…

(Man next to me interrupts saying something about an AR-15.)

O'Rourke: It's okay, let's please let her finish.

Me (turning to the man next to me): I don't have my AR-15 today, I have my Glock.

Man: Well you shouldn't have it.

Me: Don't worry sir, I have your back.

Me (turning towards O'Rourke again): Um, anyway, I want to know how you're going to legislate that because a criminal by defense (I meant definition), breaks the law. So all you're going to do is restrict law abiding citizens like myself. We all know that you sir, have a criminal history…

(Crowd jeers. But hey, it's the truth. O'Rourke had been arrested for burglary.)

Me: And I understand that burglars do not like armed defense.

O'Rourke: It's okay.

Me: Yes, sir. Burglars do not like armed defense, yet that is a right that we have that shall not be infringed in America.

I was done asking my question.

I stood there a bit numb. O'Rourke started blathering about a false assumption about all men being evil. I couldn't focus until another question came from the audience asking O'Rourke if he'd consider expanding his planned weapons ban beyond the two he already included because the guns he described weren't necessarily the ones used in the mass shootings. O'Rourke replied that he would be open to that too.

Of course, he would be.

As I started to leave, many in the crowd cussed at me. But not everyone. There were a dozen or so people who found their way over and thanked me for speaking up. They'd come to the rally for the same reason I did and let me know they supported everything I'd said.

A plainclothes police officer found me and said his chief told him to safely escort me back to my car. I truly was thankful for that, and as we walked to the car, the officer quietly told me, "Ma'am, we just want you to know how much we appreciated your words today." Another police officer chimed in to let me know he agreed.

I felt valued. I felt heard. And it felt good.

As I was driving back home, unknown to me at the time, the conservative website, *The Daily Wire*, picked up the video of my exchange at the rally and posted it on social media. Dana Loesch, a radio host and former spokesperson for the National Rifle Association, retweeted their post.

It went viral. Millions saw it and liked what I had to say.

The next day, I went to a gun show. A lady there recognized me from the video and thanked me for saying what I said and for sticking up for our Constitutionally protected rights. She started to cry and gave me a big hug. Then more of the people there came around, curious about who I was and what I had done. It seemed as if the gun show's theme quickly became that I'd stood at a Beto O'Rourke rally and defended our gun rights.

I may have been an opinionated person before, but this was the first time in my life that expressing my opinion ever made an impact on a large group of people.

The media storm after that rally was so fervent, it made the news coverage we got with Shooters Grill pale in comparison. I was interviewed by Fox News and national newspapers, with other media outlets soon following.

I was officially the mom who told Beto, "Hell no."

Those words turned into a national rallying call for our Second Amendment rights.

I now had a voice.

What was I going to do with it?

★ ★ ★ CHAPTER 16 ★ ★ ★

My Rights Don't End
Where Your Feelings Begin

A few days later, I was putting in a full day at Shooters Grill when a customer mentioned that Aspen's city council would be holding two meetings to discuss a proposed ban on open carry in city buildings and parks. The first of those meetings was that night, and the public could speak.

Though I wasn't running for office or anything, I was amped to get involved. There was still a buzz about my encounter with Beto O'Rourke, and I wanted to ride that momentum to voice concern that gun rights were being threatened. That afternoon, another concerned mom and I drove the seventy miles to Aspen to attend the city council meeting.

I'd never been to a formal government meeting before—much less to speak about guns—and had no idea what to expect. I didn't know their protocol, but the public was invited to speak, and I planned to take advantage of the opportunity. The same nervous but determined feeling I had at the O'Rourke rally came back, and I felt a pit in my stomach. When I walked into the city council chamber, I was still in my full Shooters Grill uniform—t-shirt, jeans, and a Glock 26 pistol in a custom-made leather holster on my thigh. Thirty or forty people were there, including reporters and the five council members.

When it was my turn to speak, I was invited to come up and take a seat at the table facing the council. I introduced myself and then used the limited time you're afforded to debunk the idea that somehow anyone in a government building would be made safer following the passage of their new ordinance. I explained that any criminal would simply be empowered if restrictions were placed on law-abiding citizens, who would now be unable to protect themselves—and that included me should I visit Aspen. The council listened as I explained they didn't have the authority to infringe on the Second Amendment and that they weren't above the supreme law of the land—the United States Constitution.

It took a few minutes to make my statement, and I wrapped it up by telling the council their proposal to disarm people was silly and shouldn't go any further. I thanked them for listening, but as I prepared to leave, council member Skippy Mesirow asked me to stay. He said he had an important message to share. So, in the span of a few days, I was again face-to-face with a politician in a public exchange over gun rights.[11]

> Councilman Skippy Mesirow: If I may, I want to thank you for coming this evening. I respect that you have a perspective. I respect your right to feel safe around your family and to protect yourself, etcetera. But I just want to share a bit of my perspective and my experience. Not for response, but just so you can hear it.

---

[11] Aspen City Council. Minutes, September 23, 2019. https://records.cityofaspen. com/WebLink/DocView.aspx?id=1957545&dbid=0&repo=LFRecords

Me: I may have a response.

Councilman Skippy Mesirow: When you walked in the door, I immediately noticed the firearm on your leg. All of my attention went there. I felt a wash of fear come over me. I began to… (Audience quiet gasps and murmurs)…It's true. It's absolutely true. I began to wonder. I don't know you; I assume you have the best of intentions, but I don't know, right? Um, my thoughts immediately go to where do I hide, where do I run, how do I get…please, all of this, the consequence of this was a complete shift in energy and focus, at least for me, to the point where I was, I take notes on all of this stuff so I can review afterwards, I don't even know what the first part (inaudible) was and that's something that is important to consider. So, I just want to share that with you.

Me: I'm sorry that your concentration level is that small.

(audience subdued laughter)

Councilman Skippy Mesirow: I don't need a response.

Audience Member 1: I felt safer when she walked in the room.

Audience Member 2: I felt safer.

Audience Member 1: I felt safer.

Me: Would you have had those same feelings…

Councilman Skippy Mesirow: I would ask you to have the same level of respect...

Me: (Standing up to leave) My rights do not end where your feelings begin. I appreciate you all.

And so, for me, the first meeting ended, but there was so much more to say. Council member Mesirow, in a rather succinct fashion, had just made the liberal case for safe spaces, the restriction of free speech, and the criminalization of our God-given rights. He was no different from Beto O'Rourke—making a public declaration that strikes against the very core of who we are as a free society. He also personified the weak yet elitist attitude you see in all the liberal politicians.

Mesirow was triggered by the mere sight of a diminutive woman carrying a gun. And because he was afraid, he thinks you should be too. I wasn't menacing. I merely showed up to a city council meeting to voice concern that Aspen was blatantly attempting to take away our Second Amendment rights. Yet, Mesirow admittedly "felt a wash of fear."

Was Mesirow also afraid of free speech? The Left wants to take that from you too. They're very good at silencing any opposing viewpoint—any opinion with which they disagree. When I told Mesirow I might want to respond to him, he preemptively shut me down. Before he even started to make his point about guns, he made clear that I wasn't to speak, that he had no interest in what I said to say. He wasn't interested in informed debate. No. People who live in their safe spaces don't like criticism. They don't like to be challenged. They're all for diversity of everything, except diversity of thought. No one is allowed to disagree. But if you do, they'll seek a safe space to protect themselves from the horror of words.

Let me be clear, people like Aspen Council Member Mesirow, or anyone else, have no right whatsoever to infringe upon the rights granted to us by God and by the Constitution of the United States of America. When someone's been elected to a political office—be it city council or the presidency—they're not empowered to lord over and trample on anyone's rights. In fact, it's the exact opposite. Their job is to protect those rights. Maybe Skippy Mesirow, and others like him, should sit down with a copy of the Constitution and think about what it says.

Here's a question. What would be accomplished by eliminating open-carry laws? The answer? Nothing. Think about that council meeting. When I walked in, there was no armed security. There was nothing in place at city hall to stop a gunman from entering the building. If some bad guy with a gun walked into that chamber, the only thing that would have stopped them was a good guy with a gun. If you take away the right to bear arms, it's open season on law-abiding people. The irony of Mesirow saying he was afraid when he saw my gun is that he was actually *safer* with me there.

So, that first Aspen council meeting was quite the experience. By the time the second one made the schedule, I was more fired up than before. For several days before the meeting, I meticulously prepared, even making up note cards to bring. I wanted to be sure my position was supported by plenty of facts and figures. At the heart of it was the unmitigated fact that taking guns away from law-abiding people makes them less safe.

To make my point, I brought up a news story about a local Aspen crime spree, and as you'll see, for one council member, it hit home.

A few months before the meeting, headlines in Aspen trumpeted the recent arrest of Yuri Ognacevic, a thirty-eight-year-old man charged in connection with two purse snatchings and a concession stand robbery.

What made the case noteworthy was twenty years earlier, Ognacevic was part of a teenage gang known then as "Aspen's Dirty Dozen"—a crew of twelve teens that committed armed robberies and burglaries for the better part of 1999. Ognacevic served jail time for a host of crimes, including burglary, vehicle theft, and armed robbery.

My point was, nothing the council was trying to legislate would stop the criminal, but it would make a citizen like me less safe. And in the case of a purse snatcher, if I was made to stop carrying my gun in the open and forced to conceal it in a purse—as many women do—there might be unintended consequences, like having the gun stolen by an actual criminal.

It wasn't lost on the locals in attendance, or on council member and former Aspen mayor, Rachel Richards, where my comments were heading. She most assuredly didn't want anyone talking about the Aspen Dirty Dozen.

Why?

As it turned out, Richards's son, Jacob Richards, was a member of the Dirty Dozen and played a central role in their crime spree. He reportedly worked at a grocery store the gang robbed and gave the crew the key to a home where he worked, which they robbed. Jacob was later arrested driving a vehicle stolen from that house. The crime spree netted the Dirty Dozen quite a bounty, including three shotguns and a 9mm handgun.

So, here we were in the Aspen council chambers, where a current council member, whose own son had been in a violent, armed gang, was telling law-abiding citizens when, where, and how they could use their own legally owned firearms. How rich.

Midway through my remarks, the current mayor cut me off. Was I too personal? Did I hit a nerve?

The Aspen city council went on to pass their open-carry restrictions.

Aspen might be a small town—its population is barely over 7,000—but its council is a stark reminder of how, on even the most local level, agenda-driven politicians and bureaucrats, rooted in fear, want to strip you of your rights.

Safe spaces and the heavy hand of government were alive and well in Council Member Skippy Mesirow's world. He's winning and all of us are losing. I was truly amazed at the level of fear, ignorance, and lack of any compassion toward law-abiding gun owners shown by either Beto O'Rourke or the Aspen city council. Their naked hypocrisy is a sight to behold. O'Rourke has been arrested for both burglary and driving under the influence, and, as I've noted, Council Member Richards's son was part of a notoriously violent gang. Yet, these people think they're the arbiters of morality, decency, and safety, the ones who can set us straight and lead us into being a safer society?

The best thing O'Rourke did was say out loud what we all knew—they weren't going to stop until they took our rights and guns away.

The question I had—who was going to stick up for our rights?

I had a lot more to think about after these few weeks.

TO RUN OR NOT TO RUN? THAT IS THE QUESTION

CHAPTER 17

Time to Go to Washington?

I'm a spontaneous person.

I know, big surprise. Admittedly, my spontaneity sometimes gets me into trouble, but sometimes it works out well. In the days and weeks following the Aspen city council meetings, I'd been thinking a lot about politics and just how involved I should get. I'd challenged Beto O'Rourke. I'd challenged the National Popular Vote compact. I'd challenged the Aspen city council. I'd earned praise from Dinesh D'Souza. Clearly, the path was leading me somewhere. But beyond all of these things, I thought a lot about how lackadaisical Representative Scott Tipton had been when I asked him to get involved in an issue that he should have considered to be of paramount importance. If a sitting United States congressman doesn't care enough to stand up and fight for your rights, then maybe it's time to find another congressman—and upon further thought, maybe that congressman, or woman, should be me.

After many sleepless nights, in November 2019, every spontaneous part of me said it was time to run for Congress.

This was all so very unlikely, but I truly believe it was God's plan all along. Jayson and I opened a restaurant, not knowing at the time how it would create so many opportunities beyond its four walls. Shooters Grill opened doors into the political arena I wouldn't have seen otherwise.

The right to bear arms as guaranteed in the Constitution wasn't just important to me or to my pistol-packing servers. It was important to millions of Americans. I couldn't sit idly by while Establishment politicians worked to take them away.

Every day at the restaurant, I met patriotic people who believed in freedom and America's place as a shining beacon on a hill. I'd always felt a sense of patriotism, and my life experiences had brought me to this place—a place where I'd cultivated a deep belief in life, liberty, personal responsibility, and self-determination. As a true believer in conservatism, I was growing increasingly concerned about the direction of our country.

Every day, I'd meet like-minded Americans who expressed their concerns about the liberal indoctrination of our children through the public school system, the mainstream media that refused to cover the news in a non-biased way, and the politicians who failed to solve problems, politicians more concerned with interfering in our lives. Both Colorado and the United States had a glaring lack of leadership.

Liberals were taking over our state and threatening our very way of life.

Many of the people I spoke with every day lived through tough times. It seemed that, here in Colorado, we didn't experience the economic recoveries other states did. During the good times, Shooters Grill would be packed with gas patch workers coming. Now, that rarely happens. The chatter from the ones who still came centered on how the Obama administration and Colorado's liberal environmentalists were doing everything they could to destroy our fossil fuel economy.

I shared an admiration for Senator Ted Cruz of Texas with many of the Shooters customers. He wasn't shy about calling out liberals, which was refreshing given it seemed so many other Republicans tried appeasing them instead. Senator Cruz wasn't shy about speaking up about the importance of God and guns. That was definitely okay with us.

And then there was the game changer who had gotten the attention of a lot of people who normally would try to ignore politics. New York billionaire Donald Trump announced he'd be entering the 2016 Presidential race. It was a no-brainer for me to support him. Here was an outsider, a successful businessman—a person who would stand up for ordinary Americans. With Ted Cruz in the Senate and Donald Trump as the President, sign me up!

I was MAGA from day one. "Make America Great Again" perfectly summarized what my customers and I were hungry for. Trump spoke a political language we could all understand. He was willing to stand up for working-class Americans. I could identify with Senator Cruz's conservative values and consider myself a huge fan. That said, Donald Trump as an outsider seemed like the right person for the job at the right time for our country. I even ordered a full cardboard cutout of him wearing a MAGA hat.

President Trump never stopped standing up for working Americans and our shared values. Despite the slings and arrows that liberals fired at him every single day for the duration of his presidency, Donald Trump never wavered in his resolve to make America great—and to keep it great.

With the President as my inspiration, I grew more resolute than ever to help take on the liberals and defend our rights here in Colorado. I'd embraced shades of activism over the last year—signature-gathering for the petition to repeal the National Popular Vote compact, speaking out for the Second Amendment at rallies and going to gun shows, challenging

Beto O'Rourke, giving that speech in Washington state—but where was all of this leading me? What was next for the activist in me?

As I pondered these questions, President Trump seemed to have taken some bad advice and weakened his stance on gun rights. He now supported a ban on bump stocks for guns and was talking about supporting red flag laws. The president was on a path to losing a very important part of his voter base and might not have even realized it.

I loved President Trump, but my friends and customers were growing dissatisfied. They were ready to hop off the Trump Train if he didn't defend their gun rights. Some complained he was doing more harm to the Second Amendment than President Obama ever did. I was worried and wanted to help.

My enthusiasm and earnestness were high, so high that I was naive enough to believe I could land a meeting with President Trump to straighten him out on all this. I knew he was being given bad advice in Washington, DC, by the very same RINOs (Republican in Name Only) that all of us were complaining about. Hey, I may not have been realistic in thinking I'd land a meeting, but at least I was thinking big.

Meanwhile, one of the volunteers with the National Popular Vote repeal reached out to me to attend a strategy session in Denver with Republican state party members and conservative activists. There would be people from the Trump victory team there. Surely they needed to hear our concerns, regardless of what this meeting was about. I accepted the invite because this was a good start to getting the President of the United States to Rifle to hear what his supporters had to say.

So, a group of us went up to Denver, and it took no time at all to realize we didn't fit in. I got the sense many in the room didn't know who we were or why we were there. The Colorado GOP talked a lot about election strategy and how to get out the vote, but not a lot about

President Trump. The things I had to say fell on deaf ears. The drive back to Rifle was long and disappointing. On the drive, I thought about how I could be part of the solution.

What could I do to support all the people I cared about here at home? How could I get involved more with the MAGA movement? There were plenty of people I knew who didn't want to get directly into politics but needed a voice at the table. They weren't heard at that GOP meeting. Should I be bold enough to run for Congress and be that voice? Whoa boy, there was a spontaneous idea that could get me into trouble. I figured I'd better bounce that off a few people first and pray on it. A long talk with God is always a good thing.

So, that's what I did. I talked with Jayson. He listened intently as I shared my concerns about how I believed the people of Rifle needed more of a voice. I told him that I thought I should run for Congress. Without even a hint of hesitation, Jayson told me to go for it.

It was as simple as that. That is one more reason why I love him so much, although there was a small part of me that wondered if he was just telling me what I wanted to hear.

So, with my decision made, I circled back with my friend who'd invited me to that GOP meeting in Denver. She was heavily involved with local politics, and she thought I was being too aggressive. "Slow down," she said. She advised me to run for the local school board or the county commission or even state representative. Sure, those are all worthy aspirations, but I was trying to help MAGA, not sort out local zoning laws.

Around this time, one of my uncles came up from Florida to visit family nearby. We met up at Shooters and had a long talk. I filled him in on where my head was at and told him all the things I'd been doing over the last year as an activist. He looked at me and said I'd be the perfect

Republican response to AOC. He absolutely loved the idea of me running for Congress.

Jayson and my uncle may have been supporters of a congressional run, but the local politicos—not so much. Many of them gave me similar advice as my friend about starting out slow. They said it was too late anyway to launch a successful congressional campaign. As you've no doubt learned by now, whenever I'm told I can't do something, I set out to prove them wrong. I had a friend who taught concealed weapons permit classes at Shooters who said exactly what I needed to hear—that AOC had proven there was a place for everyday citizens to run for Congress. He believed I'd do great.

I was still undecided, though. Between the advice of my friends, the doubt expressed by local party members, and what my family had to say, it was mental ping-pong. This was a strange place to be since I'm typically quite spontaneous.

I had several long talks with my pastor and prayed. What was my purpose? I thought of all the negatives. How could I possibly overcome all of the challenges that would come my way? My background, upbringing, lack of formal education, and run-ins with the law were sure to make this impossible. How would all of the people that meant the most to me—my husband, kids, mother, grandmother—handle this? Sure, they said they would support my decision, but how would it affect them? And what would happen to my restaurant?

Every conversation I had with myself always came back to the same thing—Who would speak up for us? If not me, then who? Our current congressman, Scott Tipton, wasn't getting the job done. Everyone said he was a nice guy, but it was my experience he was failing to speak up for us.

I truly believed conservatives were in a battle with liberals for the heart and soul of our country. As I've made clear, there was absolutely no way I'd allow my children to grow up in a socialist nation.

This decision would be so life-changing, I just had to pray more before I could make it. Was I being too spontaneous? After much prayer and consideration, I came to the conclusion that God had given me a spontaneous personality for a reason, and I should embrace it. It was spontaneity that led me to buy Shooters Grill. It was spontaneity that had me tell a rising political star to his face that "hell no" he wasn't taking away our guns. God made me uniquely me, and spontaneity was a part of that. He gave me a voice, and I was going to use it.

I was going to run for the United States Congress.

CHAPTER 18

Two Trips to Washington

By early December 2019, I was prepared to officially launch my campaign. *The Daily Sentinel* in Grand Junction is the primary newspaper in the 3rd Congressional District's largest market. In exchange for coverage in their Sunday edition, we offered them the exclusive on my decision to join the race.

The timing seemed ideal given the campaign's relatively late start. There were fewer than four months until the March caucus, which would determine whether I'd make it on the June primary ballot. The holidays were right around the corner, so we decided to make the announcement as soon as we could, which was in early December. There was one hiccup, though. I'd already committed to two speaking events—a gun rights rally in Denver and a fundraising event for a gubernatorial candidate in Washington state held by the same group that had me out with Dinesh D'Souza.

I couldn't back out of either event, so I spoke in Denver and then flew to Washington state, knowing my announcement would be officially made that Sunday in *The Daily Sentinel*. Life in my new political world was already getting hectic.

When I arrived in Washington, my mind was racing a thousand miles per hour. I was preoccupied with the uncertainty of what would happen following the campaign announcement. The adrenaline, excitement, and fear all came to a head when I got up to speak.

I bombed the speech, barely getting through my written notes. I'd been nervous speaking in public before, but this time, my heart was really racing. I was lost in my thoughts. The congressional run, and the uncertainty of what came with it, was a lot to process. Ironically, this embarrassing episode left me feeling uncertain about the decision I'd just made, and never before had I felt this uncertain after making a decision. It was a horrible feeling. People, as they do, told me the speech wasn't as bad as I thought it was, but I knew better.

I took a deep breath and regrouped. I thought about my motivation to run and focused on what I was trying to accomplish. I decided to stop kicking myself, enjoy the campaign, and embrace this new and uncertain world. "How would an older and wiser Congresswoman Boebert handle herself in this situation?" I thought.

The next couple of months went by with lightning speed. We were now in March, just before the Colorado caucus, and I flew to Washington, DC, to gather up support for my campaign. It doesn't sound like a big deal now, but I was a small-town girl, and until now, I'd only seen our nation's capital on television and in pictures. You'd think it would be overwhelming and that seeing the Capitol building would drive home the enormity of what I was doing. But truth be told, I had an over-whelming sense of calm—comfortable and confident about why I was running for office. Rather than get worked up about anything, I instead soaked it all in and enjoyed these first-time experiences. I never wanted to forget my first trip to Washington, DC.

After landing in town and checking into the hotel, a couple of people from my campaign team and I walked over to the Capitol building. All lit up with its bright white dome and our flag, it was more beautiful in person than I could have imagined. All I could do was smile as I was overcome by an overwhelming sense of patriotism and purpose that would continue for the entire trip.

The next day was filled with meetings to introduce me to folks who could offer support and help my campaign with fundraising. I interviewed with a whole host of people who wanted to know me better and learn what type of representative I'd be. Of course, I wanted to be aligned with those who supported conservative causes. The Club for Growth was an important meeting because they had the funding and expertise to support a true insurgent conservative candidate like me. They had plenty of questions, some of which dove deep into policy, and I, too, had a lot of policy questions. This was a great experience, and I held my own throughout the interview. Evidently, I'd done a good job because the group expressed a genuine interest in supporting the campaign and continuing the conversation when it heated up.

Next on my slate was a meeting with one of President Trump's political advisers. Our strategy was to convince him I was a true conservative worthy of the President's endorsement rather than the incumbent, Representative Tipton. We went over to the Eisenhower Executive Office Building next door to the White House but an hour before our scheduled time, our contact called to cancel. He told us the optics wouldn't be good if the President endorsed my campaign, given there was already an incumbent Republican representing our district. He emphasized that it wouldn't matter how hard we pushed, he wasn't in a position to take the meeting.

Though I was a tremendous supporter of the President, and his endorsement would have been huge—or "yuge"—I stayed calm despite the meeting cancellation. I had confidence in my campaign and our message and had an inner peace that everything would work out.

Once we'd made the rounds inside the beltway, we decided to see the monuments and memorials and take in everything around DC. We stopped in front of the White House to take pictures and then went to the nearby Trump International Hotel for dinner. This was a blast. What a fun day. The more time we spent there, the more I daydreamed about what the future might hold.

When I saw the Lincoln Memorial, it seemed much, much bigger than I'd ever imagined. On this beautiful night, President Lincoln was lit up perfectly, and the memorial was nearly empty of tourists. In the silence, we read the inscriptions of President Lincoln's Gettysburg Address and his second inaugural speech. I stood where Martin Luther King Jr. had given his famous "I have a dream" speech and looked out at the National Mall down to the Washington Monument and the Capitol building beyond that. The experience was extraordinarily moving. I wished every student could experience history this way instead of just from a textbook.

It means so much more to be there in person.

The nearby Korean War Veterans Memorial was eerily quiet, and the experience was intensified given the lack of visitors that night. As we walked the grounds and looked at the statues, we felt honored, as though we were looking straight into the eyes of heroes. The eyes of those statues pierced you, and you felt the sacrifice those brave warriors made for future generations—they understood what it meant to secure our freedom.

By now, it had gotten late, so it was time to head back to the hotel. The Lincoln Memorial Reflecting Pool, usually filled with millions of gallons of water, was under repair, so we joined a handful of other pedestrians and walked straight down the middle of it toward the Washington Monument. That too, was surreal, thinking about how many people had gathered along the mall over the years, either in protest or celebration, of our United States of America.

I didn't want the night to end.

As my group turned in for the night, I walked over to the Supreme Court. I went to the entrance and laid my hand on the front door—it was as if you could feel the history coursing through your body. I sat down on the front steps to reflect on the day and all that I'd just seen for the first time. Sitting there, in the stillness of the night, I tried to put the magnitude of what I was trying to accomplish into perspective. It felt like a spiritual experience, which elevated my mission and sense of purpose. I determined my job was to help secure the rights and freedoms for which so many Americans had sacrificed.

Now, I was more motivated than ever. The feelings of uncertainty that had made my knees buckle months before were now gone. I felt alive! My desire to fight for freedom and prosperity was on fire.

I was going to win this race.

★ ★ ★ CHAPTER 19 ★ ★ ★

Winning a Primary

I n 2016, President Trump won Colorado's 3rd Congressional District by twelve percentage points, 52 percent to 40 percent. There was no reason for the 3rd Congressional District not to have a solidly conservative Republican representing it in Congress. I was convinced I was the right person for the job.

I was feeling confident despite not having any campaign money, running against a five-term Republican incumbent, only having seven months to unseat him in a primary, and never having run for any public office.

Before I'd announced my candidacy, I met with two members of my campaign team to discuss strategy and lay out a path to victory. Obviously, this would be a grassroots campaign by necessity. We decided I'd stay true to who I am rather than attempt to be a candidate some political consultant thought I should be. I'd visit every nook and cranny of the district to meet anyone who'd listen to my message. I would not be outworked. I also knew I'd figure out how to raise some money to further this campaign.

The team and I cobbled together a basic campaign website and Facebook page, a one-page biography handout, and we drafted a press release. On December 9, 2019, I officially announced I was running for the United States Congress. Our statement read:

> "There is a battle for the heart and soul of our country that I intend on helping win," said Lauren Boebert. "I'm running for Congress to stand up for our conservative values, address our current representatives' failed promises, and put far-left Democrats back in their place. Alexandria Ocasio-Cortez, the Squad and the rest of these left-wing lunatics are taking a wrecking ball to our country while our current representative stays utterly silent," Lauren said. "Hard-working, patriotic Americans like you and me don't want the Green New Deal and socialized medicine. Every time AOC and the rest of the Squad pipes up with another crazy idea I will remind them that our belief in God, Country and Family are what built the United States of America into the greatest nation the world has ever known."

As you'd expect, an announcement that someone was challenging a five-term incumbent generated plenty of media coverage. It also helped that I'd gained some notoriety with the Beto O'Rourke confrontation. Representative Tipton didn't respond to my announcement—at least not publicly—and the media essentially gave me zero chance of beating him. Local pundits were quick to point out Tipton had successfully fended off previous primary challengers with ease.

Eleven days after my campaign announcement, on December 20, President Trump officially endorsed Tipton. Truthfully, because he had that endorsement, I believe Tipton thought the race was over before it began. I remember feeling disappointed about the endorsement, but I also convinced myself President Trump would never have given it if he was aware of what was going on in our district. And had the President known how much I supported both him and his MAGA agenda, he surely would have endorsed me instead. Both my website and Facebook page proudly declared I was a pro-Trump Republican and would continue to be, with or without his endorsement.

The campaign calendar was tight. The Colorado Caucus was in March and would determine the delegates for a Republican assembly in April, where the delegates would vote for the candidates who'd be on the June 30 primary ballot. I had several months to organize supporters to attend the caucus meetings, be selected to attend the assembly, and to vote me onto the ballot. If I didn't get 30 percent of the delegates, my campaign would be over. I had a whole lot of handshaking and baby-kissing to do, meaning I had to get out and meet with the people of the district, and given its size, that would be easier said than done.

Colorado's 3rd Congressional District is massive. It touches three of Colorado's four borders, covering twenty-six counties and encompassing nearly half of the state's landmass. It's a rural district where the key economic drivers are mining, farming, and ranching. The two largest towns are Grand Junction and Pueblo. Telluride is also part of the 3rd Congressional District, so traveling between the cities requires driving over snow-covered mountain passes. I was happy to do it because I'm at my best when connecting directly with people.

I shared my message everywhere—in big cities and small towns— like Delta, Mancos, Cortez, Durango, Meeker, and Alamosa. If a town had even a handful of people, I'd drive there, share my story, ask for campaign volunteers, and ask if they'd chip in a few bucks for the cause.

I encouraged all of them to go to the March caucus and become a delegate to the April convention.

Early on I could tell a lot of Republicans were as hungry as I was for new leadership. There was a general agreement among them that Tipton was friendly enough but wasn't a strong enough voice for conservatives. I made the case that we were in a battle with socialists and needed a fighter motivated by freedom who would stand up to them. America wouldn't become a socialist nation if I had anything to say about it. Tipton may have been the one on the Colorado ballot, but AOC was my real opponent.

There was a challenge in educating the Republican base that even though Tipton campaigned as a fiscal conservative, he didn't always vote that way. He wasn't in the media all that often and wasn't very active in the district, so Tipton was quietly getting a pass from Republicans who weren't paying the same kind of attention to his voting record as I was.

While I was out on the trail, campaigning and giving interviews with conservative media outlets, Tipton was making a series of horrible votes that bolstered the point I was making about him being a RINO. In December, he voted for a 2,000-page, $1.4 trillion spending bill without there being enough time for him to read it. I put a poll on Facebook asking if anyone thought Tipton had read the bill. Ninety-eight percent said he "Pulled a Pelosi," referencing her famous remarks that she'd find out what was in the bill after it got passed.

In January, Tipton voted for an amnesty bill. This didn't sit well with me at all, so I responded by writing the following letter:

LAUREN
BOEBERT
CONSERVATIVE FOR CONGRESS

Representative Scott Tipton   January 5, 2020
P.O. Box 1582
Cortez, Colorado 81321

Dear Representative Tipton:

It was certainly shocking that you voted alongside Nancy Pelosi, Alexandria Ocasio-Cortez and 224 other Democrats to give amnesty to millions of illegal farmworkers and their families.

To then falsely claim, "This bill is NOT an amnesty bill" is a good indicator of why you should no longer be representing hardworking American citizens in Congress. How stupid do you believe voters are?

The Heritage Foundation called the Farm Workforce Modernization Act, "foremost an illegal immigration bill that would provide amnesty for millions of illegal agricultural workers—and their spouses and children."

Mr. Tipton, you can't fool your constituents. When you allow millions of illegal aliens to indefinitely stay in the United States legally that is called <u>amnesty</u>. When you then agreed to spend $1 billion in taxpayer funds to pay for their housing, it's downright insulting.

Let's also be clear about the far-reaching implications of your actions: your vote for amnesty undermines President Trump's border security efforts. What motivation do Democrats have to negotiate with President Trump when you have already handed them exactly what they want?

There is absolutely no way Republicans would have elected you had you been honest about your support for amnesty.

Colorado's other Republican representatives, Ken Buck and Doug Lamborn, voted against H.R. 5038. Representative Buck was correct in stating the bill, "opens the door to a massive amnesty."

I look forward to the opportunity of working alongside them in the near future.

Sincerely,

Lauren Boebert
Candidate
U.S. House of Representatives (CO-3)

This amnesty vote got the attention of former Representative Tom Tancredo, who'd spent years in Congress as a staunch supporter of border security and an opponent of illegal immigration. Tancredo agreed to record a radio spot endorsing me and gave me a boost of credibility for Republicans loyal to Tipton. Now we had an open door for conversations with people otherwise reluctant to hear me out.

I spent a lot of time telling Republicans how I became a conservative—that I was a self-taught conservative raised in a Democrat household and, if not for my life experiences, I would likely be a Democrat collecting welfare checks. Most appreciated that I'd overcome tough times, worked in the local energy business, owned my own business, and was willing to stand up to Democrats like Beto O'Rourke. They now knew that I was a strongly pro-life candidate and frequently told crowds, "Planned Parenthood can go fund themselves." Oh, one other thing they liked about me? I was unabashedly supportive of President Trump. That went a long way in MAGA country.

My stump speech resonated with audiences because it was authentic. The people who came to my meetings knew exactly where I stood on the issues and that I wasn't going to be the type of professional politician we were all getting sick of in Washington, DC. I'd tell them that even though I might be outspent, I'd never be outworked. The audiences were getting bigger, and I could tell by the reactions that I was connecting in a positive way.

We were on a roll. The campaign finally scraped together the money for a television ad with a very straightforward message:

> "Hi everyone, I'm Lauren Boebert and I want you to
> send me to Congress to help President Trump build the
> wall, drain the swamp, and stand up to all the left-wing

lunatics. I'm pro-Trump, pro-Constitution, pro-Life, pro-Guns, pro-Energy. I'm a conservative, a Republican, a mom, a business owner. I'm in this fight because freedom is a great motivator. Join me. I'm Lauren Boebert, I'm running for Congress and I approved this message."

The ads we ran on both television and radio added credibility to my candidacy heading into the caucus. I felt momentum swinging in our direction. Then a curious thing happened. Tipton decided to petition onto the June primary ballot instead of going through the assembly process, which is where the delegates from the caucus would vote. This was a big deal—Tipton had always gone to assembly, and it was clear now that he was attempting to buy his way onto the primary ballot using paid signature gatherers, rather than risk not getting the necessary 30 percent of the vote at assembly.

As the caucus approached, Tipton continued to ignore me. While he was back in DC, voting for massive stimulus bills to send people $1,200 checks, the government back in Colorado was shutting down my business. I was getting a lot of press for taking on Governor Jared Polis and defying his pandemic shutdown orders. I made sure everyone knew I was going to fight to make payroll for my staff.

For voters in the 3rd Congressional District, there was a stark contrast. I was ready to fight for freedom, take on AOC and the "squad," and join President Trump in fighting to build the wall. Tipton was a Beltway insider voting alongside Nancy Pelosi to give millions of illegal aliens amnesty, rubber-stamping massive spending bills, and trying to buy his way onto the Republican primary ballot.

My campaign was practically broke, but we had heart, grit, and press coverage nobody could buy.

Remember when that advisor for President Trump canceled our meeting? Well, he and the rest of their team could no longer dismiss us. In fact, the Trump Victory team took notice of what was happening in my race and the momentum the campaign had. It was hard not to notice the response I was getting from audiences—the enthusiasm was off-the-charts. Our supporters had something money can't buy—passion. While our campaign was rolling like a freight train, Tipton's went practically radio silent.

Good for us.

In April, Tipton decided to become the first Republican co-sponsor of what I would call the "Boulder Bailout." I waited until the primary ballots were mailed out and then attacked the bill full force, sending the following letter and launching an extremely effective "Boulder Bailout" television ad.

Representative Scott Tipton   June 5, 2020
P.O. Box 1582
Cortez, Colorado 81321

Dear Representative Tipton:

Your decision to join AOC and her Squad to bailout Boulder is as shocking as your previous decision to vote alongside Nancy Pelosi to hand amnesty to millions of illegal immigrants.

On April 7th, Boulder's Representative Joe Neguse introduced H.R. 6467. Denver's Fox 31 reported: "...Neguse introduced a bill that would provide $250 billion in relief to cities and towns below that 500,000 threshold, including Boulder...".

On April 7th AOC and her Squad (Alexandria Ocasio-Cortez, Ilhan Omar, Rashida Tlaib, Ayanna Pressley) joined the bill as original co-sponsors.

On April 14th you became the first and only Republican at that time to co-sponsor the bill, joining AOC and her Squad to bailout Boulder. Tellingly, Colorado's other Republican representatives, Ken Buck and Doug Lamborn, refused to join you.

Boulder is one of the wealthiest and liberal communities in the country. The Boulder city budget includes $6 million per year for "climate initiatives", mandates a "living wage" of more than $17 per hour for every city employee and the city's rainy-day fund that has yet to be exhausted.

You should be ashamed asking ranchers in Craig and peach farmers in Palisade and steelworkers in Pueblo to bailout Boulder. Boulder can go fund themselves.

It was your decision to join AOC and the Squad to bailout Boulder instead of crafting better legislation. It was your decision to waste taxpayer dollars on liberal bailouts. That's on you. Own it.

Sincerely,

Lauren Boebert

Lauren Boebert
Candidate
U.S. House of Representatives (CO-3)

P.S. Hiring high-priced lawyers to stop me from telling the truth about your voting record is unbecoming of your office. Please remember your oath includes protecting my 1st Amendment rights.

PAID FOR BY LAUREN BOEBERT FOR CONGRESS

Lauren Boebert for Congress • PO Box 752 Rifle, Colorado 81650 • info@LaurenforColorado.com

If there was any doubt among voters there was a contrast between the two candidates, they were squashed right then. They could choose the candidate with a track record of fighting for small businesses and who would go to Washington to take on AOC and the squad or choose the professional politician who'd find a way to join AOC and her squad to give Boulder a bailout.

I made more rounds around the district in June to get the vote out, gained some momentum with the television ad, and tried my best to give every media interview I could.

Even after the primary ballot had been mailed, Tipton's campaign was still basically off-the-grid. He refused to debate and wouldn't even say my name in public. At one campaign stop, attended by the both of us, I approached Tipton, said "Hello," and formally introduced myself. It was a brief exchange, to say the least. His campaign didn't think I had enough money or name recognition to win. Big mistake. Huge. But you can understand why they thought that—about 98 percent of the time, incumbents win because they have both money and name recognition. Tipton certainly had both.

Tipton did himself no favors and inadvertently made my points for me. He'd disrespected the delegates by bypassing the assembly process, and his voting record as of late showed he would vote with the Democrats. Tipton was not the conservative people believed him to be.

It was time to vote for a true conservative. Me.

To the extent Tipton was doing any campaigning, it was from paid staff and surrogates who'd show up at roundtable meetings with an agenda that was little more than to criticize me. I was in Aspen for one of these meetings when one of Tipton's longtime associates—triggered by my mere presence—embarrassed herself with a condescending, elitist speech that said more about her than it did me. She launched into a diatribe about how stupid and uneducated I was while making sure we all knew she had a master's degree in public administration. I just had to smile because it was obvious that I'd gotten under their skin.

This is what happens when an underdog challenges the Establishment elite. Even some members of the local Republican party and a few elected officials had no idea what to make of me. Some aggressively opposed my campaign despite rules prohibiting them from being active in the primary. It made no sense to me. Weren't we all Republicans? Their job was to support the process, including both primary candidates. Still, one county chair refused to distribute my campaign materials and posted message after message about what a horribly unprepared, underfunded candidate I was and that I'd be annihilated in the general election. He was so angry it was almost comical.

In the final couple of weeks of the primary campaign, with ballots already out and returns coming in at a steady clip, the Tipton team sent a couple of mailers out falsely attacking me as a liar. They also held a district-wide telephone town hall meeting with President Trump, who reiterated his endorsement for Tipton.

Our campaign poured every dime we had into radio and television ads, and we, too, sent out a mailer with all my stump speech points and a copy of the amnesty letter. We had volunteers relentlessly working the phones calling every likely voter to urge them to get their ballots in. We held rallies and did a social media blitz to get out the vote.

By June 30, I knew we'd done everything we could to win the primary, and it was now out of my hands. It was up to the voters to decide whether I was the person they wanted to represent them.

There was an election night party in Grand Junction attended by our team and other Republican campaigns in various state races. The results started to roll in a little past 7:00, and as each county total went up on the board, it became increasingly apparent I was going to win.

My phone started ringing off the hook. Senator Cory Gardner and Representative Ken Buck, the head of the Colorado Republican Party, called to congratulate me. In my excitement, I accidentally hung up on Republican Minority Leader Kevin McCarthy and had to call him back. Over the next twenty-four hours, I'd get calls from other members of Congress and Vice President Mike Pence, who called me from Air Force Two and wished me the best of luck.

To his credit, Tipton called to congratulate me and wish me luck. He was gracious and kind. I was proud of the fact that I never attacked him personally during the campaign and was only critical of his voting record and the way he ran his congressional office, both of which I think are always fair game.

Then came the greatest call of them all.

The phone rang, I picked it up, and there on the other end was the familiar voice of the forty-fifth President of the United States, Donald J. Trump. Are you kidding me?! He called to tell me he was looking forward to having a fighter join him in Washington, DC—one who'd help take on all the crazy liberals. "Mr. President," I told him, "I'm very much looking forward to joining that fight."

To the people of the 3rd Congressional District, I had a few things to say too. I sent out a statement saying:

"Our freedom and our Constitutional rights are on the ballot this November and Republicans just sent a loud and clear message that they want me there to fight for them. I joined this race because thousands of ordinary Americans just like me are fed-up with politics as usual.

Colorado deserves a fighter who will stand up for freedom, who believes in America and who is willing to take on all the left-wing lunatics who are trying so hard to ruin our country. We are in a battle for the heart and soul of our country. I'm going to win this November because freedom is a great motivator."

The final vote count was 58,675 to 48,805. It was the first time in forty-eight years in Colorado that a candidate for Congress had upset an incumbent.

There's something to be said for the power of a message that resonates. In the primary, our campaign spent a miserly—by political standards—$130,000, stayed debt-free, and even had $10,000 left in the bank account. Our campaign was grassroots in every sense of the word, and it worked.

Now it was time to win the general election.

★ ★ ★

ONE UPSET DOWN, ONE MORE TO GO

★ ★ ★

CHAPTER 20

Dirty Pool

By no means am I your typical politician because up until becoming a United States congresswoman, I never was a politician. I certainly wasn't a typical political candidate because I'd never been a candidate before running for Congress. When you're out of the box, no one knows what to make of you—which, in my case, was a good thing because that's how I'd beaten an Establishment politician like Scott Tipton. Hopefully, the "X" factor would be a big help in the race against my next Establishment opponent, an ultra-liberal Democrat named Diane Mitsch Bush.

Our win over Tipton shocked most of the mainstream politicos. I wasn't an Establishment candidate, meaning I didn't rise through the local ranks, pay political dues, establish relationships with the media, or have a war chest full of money. In our campaign, there was no team of DC consultants or any opposition research. We'd beaten the Establishment because we had a message that resonated with voters. We were grassroots without the sense of entitlement of an Establishment politician, you know, where if you played the game correctly, you'd be anointed, much the same way Beto O'Rourke had been.

We had no wealthy donors who expected favors; no quid pro quo with any politician where "If you scratch my back, I'll scratch yours." Our campaign was run by instinct and not formula, and I'd ruffled a lot of Establishment feathers by often bypassing the media and sharing my message directly with the people I wanted to represent.

One thing I'd learned, and it was a surprise at that, was how the enemy wasn't just the other side; it could often be people in your own party. Establishment Republicans—RINOs—didn't want me to beat Tipton. They had a good thing going. Now, here was a political novice, a true conservative, an outsider spoiling it all. When I won the primary election, heads likely exploded because I didn't follow the Establishment playbook or play by any of their rules.

I'd seen the ugly side of politics in running against Tipton, but as our campaign geared up to defeat Mitsch Bush, I never could have known just how ugly it was about to get. We were also about to learn the lengths to which the biased mainstream media will go to destroy you.

My concern wasn't the media, though. It never has been. My only interest then, as it is now, was to serve the people of the 3rd Congressional District. As I did when I ran against Tipton, I hit the road to meet as many people as I possibly could, so I could share with them my message of freedom and prosperity. I promised I'd always be a strong conservative who worked for them and not the power brokers in Washington, DC, or for any special interest groups. I wanted to make it clear just exactly where I stood on the issues, so I released my Contract with Colorado, which read like this:

<u>America First.</u>

I work for you, not special interests, not Washington, D.C. Just you!

I'll always vote for a strong national defense, better care for our Veterans, stronger trade agreements, and to keep the promises we've made to our seniors. No Green New Deal, no more D.C. power grabs, always what's right for Colorado.

Constitution and Bill of Rights.

My job is to secure your rights and defend the Constitution as it is written.

I won't let them take away our guns. I'll always stand up for freedom of speech. I'm against judges who legislate from the bench. I'm against the national popular vote. Colorado's voice matters and we can't give that away to California.

Limited Government.

An entrenched federal bureaucracy with over two million federal employees who earn more and receive better benefits than Main Street is far from what our founders envisioned.

Term limits for all politicians, not just the good ones. Cap federal civilian pay and benefits to private sector levels. Give more authority to the President to take on the Deep State by firing those in the executive branch not implementing his policies.

Free Markets.

Free and fair markets work when we let them.

Fewer over-reaching regulations and more competition will deliver better outcomes. Healthcare should be personal and portable with transparent and competitive pricing. Veterans should have a private-sector option, too!

Life.

I believe life begins at conception.

Planned Parenthood can go fund themselves. They should never receive a dime of our federal tax dollars.

Liberty.

Attacks on our personal freedom must stop.

I will never vote to give away our personal freedom to socialists, globalists or other left-wing lunatics.

Watch out AOC and the Squad, here I come!

Strong Borders.

A country without borders is not a country at all.

We must enforce our current immigration laws, put a stop to sanctuary cities and build the wall.

Energy.

Energy independence is critical to our national defense and economic security.

I support an all-of-the-above strategy where the government does not choose winners and losers. Drill baby, drill!

Add new nuclear technology to the mix as a clean and efficient energy source.

Fiscal Responsibility.

The federal government doesn't have a revenue problem, it has a spending problem.

We don't need tax increases. I will introduce and vote for a Balanced Budget Amendment every year I serve in Congress.

School Choice.

Charter schools work. School choice works. Local decision making is better.

Parents know better than bureaucrats. There shouldn't even be a federal Department of Education.

Leadership.

I am a strong conservative with principles that I will always stand up for.

Of course, the Contract with Colorado was panned by Colorado's left-wing media as lacking substance. Here's a tip, if you're a conservative and the media criticizes something you're doing, then it's highly likely you're doing the right thing.

This was just the start of the media's efforts to destroy me. They had an anti-gun rights Establishment candidate in Mitsch Bush, who they desperately wanted in Washington, so they'd do just about anything to discredit me.

In the coming months, I'd learn what a political proctology exam feels like.

From the start, they'd concocted and spread false rumors, provided one-sided coverage, and did all they could to paint me as a redneck, MAGA nutcase.

The professional game of politics starts with opposition research. It's not as sinister as you might think; this allows politicians to understand their opponent's background and policy positions. But make no mistake, opposition research definitely includes "digging up the dirt," and usually no stone is left unturned—past voting records, arrest records, public business records, social media posts, tax liens, foreclosures, and everything part of your life, both public and private.

As you've already seen, my life wasn't perfect. I had a tough upbringing and made mistakes along the way. But if those were the things that made me the fighter I am today, for the leftist Establishment, they were the grist for the mill they'd use to try to destroy my candidacy.

Funny thing is, I never tried to hide anything, as so many politicians do. I believe people have the right to know about the candidates for whom they're voting. If my opponents wanted to attack me personally, go ahead. I considered my background an asset and not a liability. I'd lived a real life—one a lot of people could identify with—unlike most professional, career-politicians. So at the time, I gave no thought to what the opposition research would find. I just didn't see it as a problem.

Here's the thing, though. If the opposition doesn't find what they think they need to defeat you, they'll either make up things or try to associate you with something that will. And when they get the powerful, liberal mainstream media on their side, that's when things get really ugly.

CHAPTER 21

Fighting the Falsehoods of Fake News

F ake News is a very real thing.

Misinformation comes from everywhere—a loose cabal of political campaigns, professional activists, third-party political committees, blogs, social media, debate moderators, forum hosts, and the news media. A lot of it is political theater.

Not every news story is Fake News, and not all Fake News is aimed at Republicans, even though it often feels that way. I don't think Fake News is always intentional; sometimes a "journalist" is just bad at their job. Nevertheless, Fake News, when it rears its ugly head, is harmful and creates distrust and anger. It triggers division and stokes hyper-partisanship.

Fake News isn't limited to what you've seen or heard, it can also be the news you never hear about. Sometimes a reporter or network story will conveniently ignore a fact, a response, or a policy position and omit it from the story. What often happens—and this has happened a lot with me—is you'll engage in a lengthy and substantive conversation with a reporter about policy positions and then either never see a story published or see one published but without any policy content at all.

When mainstream media doesn't like what they're hearing, they will not report it. I can't count all the times the press has been fixated on a meaningless topic no one cares about and then hypes it up as if it's the big game changer.

A lot of this happens because political consultants will sort through the opposition research and hire a polling firm to test the strongest attacks—to gauge how, or if, their opinions will be influenced by knowing something negative about the opponent. Then they choose the most effective attacks based on the polling.

Tonight, watch the news. If you hear a Democrat talking about Russian influence or right-wing conspiracy theories, or how a candidate is too extreme for this or that, it's not organic happenstance but rather a poll-tested message they believe will change votes.

What we saw with our campaign was an effort to keep us on the defensive, which intensified as we got closer to Election Day.

Sure, we monitored television, radio, newspapers, social media, and online news outlets. Did they pick up the stuff that was out there? We even did our own polling to see how the things from my past would affect the campaign. Would my mugshots, which the opposition had photoshopped to look like "Wanted" posters, turn voters against me? We found out that most fabricated or embellished attacks are ineffective. That was one of the more reassuring things I'd learned on the campaign trail; it kept my faith that the electorate was smart enough to see through most of this political garbage.

Still, Mitsch Bush's campaign didn't care much about that. They picked up a shovel and thrust it into the dirt in the hopes of duping the electorate into voting for someone whose policies would be disastrous for Colorado.

Mitsch Bush had a health-care policy problem that didn't poll well in the 3rd Congressional District. For years, Mitsch Bush advocated for socialized medicine, going so far as to Tweet, "I absolutely support Medicare for All," and that, "The majority of Americans…are looking for more government intervention in their healthcare." I don't know what Americans she was talking with, but I don't know many who want *more* government control of their health care. Mitsch Bush championed "universal, single-payer healthcare." She even displayed a big picture on her previous campaign website of Bernie Sanders, the multimillionaire socialist, advocating for Medicare for All. In other words, Mitsch Bush had a health care policy that voters in my district didn't like.

One of the problems Mitsch Bush faced in selling her bad policy was that, unlike most Republicans, I never advocated for dismantling the Affordable Care Act (ACA), more commonly known as "Obamacare." (I did, however, criticize Republicans for failing to keep their promise to repeal and replace it.) That meant her boilerplate Democrat attack strategy wouldn't work on me. I never cast a vote against the ACA. I never said we should repeal it.

Long before the general election, I made it clear in my Contract with Colorado that health care should be personal and portable and that pricing should be transparent and competitive. To me, these are big and powerful policy points that, if instituted, would change the trajectory of rising health insurance premiums and deliver better care.

It didn't matter that my opponent was vulnerable on health-care policy because the Fake News was ready to hop in and help once her campaign machine laid down her poll-tested talking points. Suddenly, Mitsch Bush didn't support Medicare for All. Suddenly, according to her, I didn't have a health-care plan. Suddenly, I was for repealing the ACA, which would leave hundreds of thousands of Coloradans without health insurance.

Every claim levied against me was a lie.

On August 9, 2020, I issued a statement outlining all of Mitsch Bush's false claims and made clear, "I will never vote for legislation that will leave Coloradans without health coverage."

Seven days later, Fake News would strike again. *The Denver Post* made the false claim that "Lauren Boebert doesn't have a health care plan, only vague goals, and a history of criticizing the Affordable Care Act."[12] Interestingly, the article also said repealing the ACA without a replacement would leave 159,000 Coloradans without health insurance. And before the article ended, there was a direct and unchallenged quote from Mitsch Bush, falsely claiming that I had "no plan to make health-care more affordable for people in the 3rd (District), and instead she wants to take health care away from hundreds of thousands of people during a national health care and economic crisis."

If you didn't know any better, who would you vote for after reading that?

Suddenly, I was the candidate without a health-care plan who wanted to strip Coloradans of their health insurance, facts be damned. Mitsch Bush wasted no time in running attack ads on television, citing the false claims made in *The Denver Post*.

Did the paper intentionally write falsehoods? I don't think so, but it didn't matter. The damage was done. Mitsch Bush was happy to take advantage of the misinformation and roll out those attack ads.

---

[12] Wingerter, Justin. "Health care takes center stage in Colorado's 3rd Congressional race." *The Denver Post*, August 16, 2020

The Denver Post wasn't the only publication showing a one-sided bias. The paper with the largest circulation in my district did too. *The Daily Sentinel* in Grand Junction was happy to focus on health care as a central issue to my campaign, which should have been a blessing for me, but it refused to share my side of the story.

The lead political reporter for the *Sentinel* interviewed me a couple of months before the election. The first half of his interview consisted of personal questions such as my mother's need to be on welfare while she raised me, whether we moved to the Western Slope because Mom met a guy, and how old I was when I became pregnant with my first son. The second half of the interview focused on policy issues ranging from water, energy, federal lands, forest management to health care. I had high hopes for a fair article that finally covered some of my policy positions. The article came out a week later titled, "Boebert's Democratic Upbringing Questioned."[13]

Not one line of policy.

Not one.

The pathetic thing is the *Sentinel* knew my policy positions on health care. I'd sent them a letter a month before they interviewed me, where I outlined my health-care policy and how it contrasted with Mitsch Bush's. The paper refused to print it. Then when my communications director emailed to ask why, their editorial page editor replied, "After consulting with the publisher, who has the final say on these matters, the *Sentinel's* position is that we won't publish this letter. Lauren has already received ample space on our opinion pages to further her candidacy. Her campaign has access to reporters or paid political advertising to make these points. Lauren will be invited to meet with our

---

[13] Ashby, Charles. "Boebert's Democratic Upbringing Questioned." *The Daily Sentinel,* September 21, 2020

editorial board and she can make these points then, as well. Thanks for your patience."

I'd bet Mitsch Bush never got an email like that.

Some might say the *Sentinel's* response was a reasonable one—except for its one glaring falsehood. I'd already submitted three previous letters to their editor (January 10, May 13, and June 2), and none of those letters were published either. So for them to say, "Lauren has already received ample space on our opinion pages to further her candidacy," was disingenuous at best.

It got worse.

On August 30, the *Sentinel* published an editorial headlined, "A new prescription for health care costs"[14]—they wrote, "Lauren Boebert needs to explain how she would repeal the Affordable Care Act, but still keep its protections for folks with pre-existing conditions, especially given her 'get the government out of people's lives' philosophy. Diane Mitsch Bush needs to explain how innovation would be retained with the expanded role for government she advocates."

What? I'd already submitted a health-care op-ed that explained my positions, and they refused to print it. Now the *Sentinel* was trying to publicly shame me into having to explain a position I'd never taken. I never advocated for the repeal of the ACA, yet here was the *Sentinel* demanding I tell people how I would do so.

My communications director emailed the publisher, asking if he had actually seen the August 9th press release that accompanied the health-care letter to the editor. The publisher responded that he had seen it, it was his decision not to publish it, and said, "This is a political ad— consistent with her talking points on the subject. We're all looking for

---

[14] Editorial Board. "A new prescription for health care costs." *The Daily Sentinel*, August 30, 2020

substance." In other words, they just didn't like what I had to say about health care and were demanding that I either give them content to their liking or advertise with them.

Of course, the *Sentinel* had no such qualms in publishing Mitsch Bush's op-ed on health care, which they did on September 12, 2020. As you'd expect, it was all political spin loaded with lies.

What to do? I fought back.

I took out full-page ads showcasing Mitsch Bush's previous tweets advocating for socialized medicine. The ads were expensive but necessary because she was going unchallenged about her real health-care position.

Then I accepted the *Sentinel's* offer to make my health-care points at a meeting of their editorial board. I methodically went through Mitsch Bush's health-care op-ed point-by-point. After the meeting, and despite every single point I made, the *Sentinel* published another editorial that claimed, "Lauren Boebert stonewalled the *Sentinel's* editorial board and eluded virtually all of our questions."[15] Of course, they sang my opponent's praises, "Diane Mitsch Bush was much more forthcoming, answering each and every question we posed. We not only got a sense of her legislative priorities—lowering health-care costs, creating more jobs that pay a living wage and protecting public lands—but also her approach to achieving policy wins."

Wow. If you believed the *Sentinel*, Mitsch Bush was Mother Teresa and Florence Nightingale all rolled into one.

So, what really happened in that editorial meeting? I took Mitsch Bush's printed health-care editorial, added my notes in CAPS, and read it line-by-line to everybody in the room. When they tried to dismiss me by skipping ahead to move on to other subjects, I stayed the course. If I

---

[15] "Colorado District 3." *The Daily Sentinel*, October 21, 2020

wasn't going to get a fair shake on health care, I sure as heck was going to leave that meeting knowing everyone in the room knew how I felt about it.

The *Sentinel* never treated me fairly, but surely they'd cash the check if I bought ad space from them. Bottom line, they slanted the coverage because their editorial board disagreed with my politics—a cornerstone of Fake News.

CHAPTER 22

The Debates

Historically, in the 3rd Congressional District, there are two main debates held each election cycle. One is with the Pueblo Chieftain, and the other is with a non-profit coalition called Club 20 in Grand Junction. Each invited me to participate, and I immediately accepted.

However, Mitsch Bush publicly refused the Club 20 debate and told the Pueblo Chieftain she wasn't available for any of the dates they offered, even though we were both given two months' notice and offered five different days to choose from during the week of October 10th.

Any person even remotely paying attention could tell the debates were canceled because Democrat Diane Mitsch Bush refused to partici-pate. After all, it takes two participants to have a debate, right? Since I'd accepted the invitation, there was only one reasonable conclusion.

Wrong.

In the world of Fake News, it's a problem when the Democrat doesn't want to debate. Now, the Fake News was manufacturing the expecta-tion that I needed to somehow be in a debate by myself. That was such an absurd notion. Of course, Fake News would then falsely claim I was withdrawing from a debate. Here's a question—just exactly how does one withdraw from a debate that doesn't exist? Who knows? But according to the Fake News, I did just that. They ran stories with headlines proclaiming:

"Boebert Withdraws from Club 20 Debate"

"U.S. House Candidate (Boebert) Latest
to Bow Out of Club 20 Debate"

"Debates are a Sticking Point for Lauren
Boebert and Diane Mitsch Bush"

"It's Official (Boebert) Doesn't Want to Debate"

"Mitsch Bush and Boebert at Odds Over
Scheduling Debates"

"Will Candidates for Congress Meet in a Debate?"

As the election got closer and the polls showed Mitsch Bush was likely to lose, her campaign elevated their lies about me to new levels. Her debate withdrawal strategy failed so miserably that she started issuing press releases lying about her willingness to debate. In one gem of a Tweet, Mitsch Bush wrote, "Let's get one thing straight: I've accepted 4 debates/forums to have a discussion about the specific issues facing CO-3. Boebert still hasn't accepted ANY of those challenges. What's she afraid of?" But here's the thing about liberals like Mitsch Bush: their schemes almost always end up blowing up in the faces. After another

Tweet where she wrote, "How can Boebert get the job if she won't show up and answer the tough questions?"—her reckoning was coming.

I wouldn't show up? Please. If a lie like that remains unchecked, then, really, where are we as a country? But the good news, someone did check it—the debate moderator herself. Edie Sonn replied to Mitsch Bush's tweet and called her out for lying. "Rep MB, I've always been a supporter of yours," wrote Sonn, "But you can't make this statement seriously. I was supposed to moderate your debate at Club 20 and you declined to participate because of COVID. We did them in a TV studio, distanced, no audience. No Bueno."

Finally, someone exposed the truth. Not only had Mitsch Bush lied about who wouldn't debate, but the debate moderator herself also called her out on it—despite being one of her supporters!

If you're paying attention, you'll note a pretty big problem here, besides the lying, of course. Club 20 had not chosen a neutral moderator. They'd picked someone who openly supported one of the candidates. That in itself should have been a headline. Sonn exposing Mitsch Bush's lie should have been one, too. But with Fake News, never.

Fortunately, my campaign was able to get a screen capture of the Twitter exchange before it was deleted, and we turned it into another full-page advertisement. Go, team!

CHAPTER 23

Wait. What's QAnon?

In May 2020, I was interviewed by *The Steel Truth,* an online news program, and asked whether I knew about the "Q" movement. I didn't know a lot about it, but, yes, I'd heard of it because Mom had heard a little something about it. They asked if I thought Q was a bad thing, and I told them I didn't think so, but I hoped that what I had heard about Q was real, if for no other reason than it could only mean America was getting stronger and people were returning to conservative values.

The key here is I'd only "heard" about Q. That's it, and I made that clear during the interview. Mom told me she'd heard government employees were working to undermine President Trump and his agenda and that a government insider using the name "Q" was working to expose the truth about the so-called "deep state." That's it.

Anyone trying to expose the truth responsibly, whatever that may be, certainly sounded good to me. And the chief executive of the United States should have the full faith and support of those who work for him. Bureaucrats shouldn't undermine the President's policies; they should help enact them. This certainly wasn't a radical notion. The inspector general for the Department of Justice, Michael Horowitz, had investigated concerns that President Trump had been undermined by government insiders. He produced hundreds of pages of investigative work related to these claims against the "deep state." United States Attorney General William Barr was also investigating claims of deep state activity that questioned the motivations behind the highest officials at the FBI and how they may have spied on President Trump's 2016 campaign.

I never mentioned Q again after *The Steel Truth* interview, and I never made any references or comments to being a Q follower. I never paid much attention to conspiracy theories, and I sure wasn't a conspiracy theorist. Any rational person would think that would be the end of that. But politics isn't rational, and the Fake News machine kicked into high gear.

Suddenly, Fake News was falsely accusing me of being a QAnon follower and a conspiracy theorist. Huh? The media said if I was associated with QAnon, then how could anyone vote for me? The problem was I had no idea what they were talking about.

A reporter from *The New York Times* called me and asked if I was a QAnon follower, and of course, I told him I wasn't. At one point during the interview, I had to interrupt him to say he seemed to know a lot more about QAnon than I did. The Democratic Congressional Campaign Committee (DCCC) began a harassment campaign on Twitter. I tweeted back, "Hey @DCCC, QAnon=Fake News. Not a follower. Is this all you've got?"

USA Today called for an interview, and I made it unequivocally clear, "I'm not into conspiracies. I'm into freedom and the Constitution of the United States of America. I'm not a follower." I told the local Fox station, "I'm not a follower of QAnon, my mom is not a supporter of QAnon, she just talked to me about it one time." A *Politico* profile piece managed to back up what I'd said, "Her campaign has since said repeatedly that Boebert does not support the QAnon theory…"

As much as I refuted the claims, the more they were printed and turned into campaign attacks. I felt like I was playing whack-a-mole against these stupid stories, but there were more moles than my communications director and I could keep up with. Everywhere I turned, there was another story trying to tie me to QAnon. As usual, with the Fake News and liberals in general, when they can't win with their policies, they turn to disinformation and attacks.

Funny thing was none of the voters I'd met on the campaign trail ever brought up QAnon. This was such a non-issue despite the Fake News obsession with it.

I'd later learn just how obsessed they were with tying, not just me, but all conservatives to QAnon.

After I defeated Mitsch Bush, I was getting ready for freshman orientation at the Capitol with some of my new colleagues and learned many of them across the country had the same experience with the same false attacks. They'd be out campaigning, and then suddenly, Fake News would tag them as a QAnon supporter.

Representative Burgess Owens was running his campaign in Utah and appeared on a podcast, in which he spoke at length about his campaign and his faith as a Christian. He never once mentioned QAnon—not once. Yet, that didn't stop *The Salt Lake Tribune* from publishing an article with the headline, "Burgess Owens appears on a QAnon conspiracy theory-linked program." Interestingly, in the article's second paragraph, the *Tribune* gave attribution to Media Matters for America for the story. For those unaware, Media Matters is a liberal activist group funded by billionaire George Soros, a man who's spent quite a bit of his wealth trying to destroy America as we know it.

With the Fake News, facts don't matter, and even if a story is proven to be false, they revel in planting that first seed and are hopeful that the story will spread online and everywhere. A story linking Owens to QAnon also ran in Utah's *Daily Herald*.

Owens gave a radio interview at around that same time in which he did mention QAnon. He made a good point about how we should take a deeper look at whatever the Left calls a "conspiracy" because it's probably something they're trying to hide. He went on to say about QAnon, "Whatever this other group is, I have no idea."

That didn't stop the *Tribune* from publishing another story linking Owens to QAnon, this one headlined, "Ben McAdams Demands Burgess Owens Disavow QAnon after he suggested the conspiracy theory may have merit." McAdams was Owen's Democratic challenger.

See how Fake News works, now? Guilt by any semblance of association, funded by leftist organizations, escalated by dishonest candidates, validated by established news outlets, and turned into campaign attacks to influence votes.

As I am writing this, Nancy Pelosi is accusing Republican House Leader Kevin McCarthy of being associated with Q.

To be crystal clear, that too is Fake News.

As our campaign pushed forward, our communications director would often be contacted by "reporters" from publications she'd never heard of. They'd ask for a comment about some salacious accusation they'd heard about me, then say, "I'm on deadline." That's a well-worn reporter technique to elicit a defensive answer along the lines of, "I didn't beat my wife," which instantly presents a candidate in a bad light. This agenda-driven approach is not news reporting; it's attack seeding to intentionally flood the internet with unchallenged negative stories—and it limits access to candidates by lesser-known but legitimate news outlets.

This happens with the mainstream media too. *Aspen Daily News* is a legitimate small-town news publication in the Third Congressional District. Whenever they'd ask, I was happy to discuss the campaign with them, even though it's not a secret *Aspen Daily News* is a left-leaning paper that would never endorse me. I generally had an okay relationship with the paper, except with one of their columnists, Wendle Whiting, who seemed to have a special level of vitriol toward me. I'd later learn this was the same Wendle Whiting who logged into Mitsch Bush's Zoom campaign briefing and introduced himself to the group by saying, "I despise Lauren Boebert."

How's that for fair and balanced journalism?

Look at Whiting's Twitter feed sometime. It's nice to know that I live rent-free inside his head.

As the campaign shifted into high gear and made its way toward Election Day, I started hearing about a new political action committee, Rural Colorado United (RCU), formed to oppose the campaign. Reporters would ask me to comment on accusations made toward me by RCU. They'd often quote the group's co-founder, a man named George Autobee, who somehow got the media to believe he was just a folksy, retired military veteran from southern Colorado who was taking up a grassroots stand against my campaign.

It wasn't until after the election that most of us learned Autobee is a highly trained, well-funded Democrat political operative. He worked for Hillary Clinton, Barack Obama, and a former Democrat governor of Colorado. Autobee was also a longtime supporter of the very person I was running against, Mitsch Bush. In 2018, he appeared in her campaign ads, attacking her Republican opponent on military veteran issues. Now, he was after me.

Autobee didn't do this by himself. According to a post-election interview published in 2021, he was approached to form a PAC and to be the face of a well-funded group whose sole purpose was to raise hundreds of thousands of dollars to defeat me. See the deception the Left uses? The entire time we were running the campaign, voters heard about veteran George Autobee and his modest upstart, Rural Colorado United—when in fact, it was all smoke and mirrors. The Left can't win on the strength of their positions, so they have to resort to this kind of deception.

Chances are that when the next election rolls around, you won't see Fake News referring to George Autobee as a well-funded, far-left, former Hillary Clinton and Barack Obama political operative. But at least it would be true.

Fake News seeks to shape our country, and it'll have long-lasting implications for how politics are carried out in our country.

Here's the thing, though: I still won the election.

CHAPTER 24

Shut Down but Not Out

I beat Mitsch Bush by six points.

More than half of the voters in the 3rd Congressional District decided that a working mom—a no-nonsense, political outsider was the best person to represent them in Washington. I had a message that connected, and I embodied what I believe the Founding Fathers had envisioned for Congress—a citizen representative.

Career-politicians don't work for you. They work for special interests and to enrich themselves. If you don't believe that, ask yourself how so many politicians in Washington became millionaires working on a government salary.

One of the reasons why I believe so many people connected with our campaign was because I was actually out there, in the district, meeting them. Remember, this entire campaign was run during a pandemic. Draconian lockdowns and widespread fear thwarted any normalcy of the process. Mitsch Bush chose to stay home for the most part. She'd held only "virtual" campaign events and, not unlike Joe Biden, thought the best strategy was to stay in the basement—so to speak.

While Mitsch Bush stayed home, sent out postcards and mailers, and ran television ads, I was out there, in the district, pounding the pavement and meeting the voters. How can you expect to get someone excited about your message if you never even meet them? We'd been criticized for holding meet-and-greet events where many of the attendees were without masks and doing such dastardly things as hugging or shaking hands. But whether someone attended one of our events, or wore a mask if they did, that's a choice they made for themselves. We didn't mandate anything. Freedom is precious, and nowhere in the Declaration of Independence or the Constitution does it say, "We are endowed by a Creator with certain unalienable rights, that among these are life, liberty, and the pursuit of happiness—unless there's a respiratory virus with a near 99-percent rate of survival, then forget it."

What we saw during the peak of the pandemic was overreaching, tyrannical politicians using it to assume power. And it came at every level—even tiny town mayors, county judges, and city councils thought COVID-19 empowered them to lord over the citizenry. We didn't see this sort of power grab during the H1N1 swine-flu outbreak of 2009 and 2010. Of course, Barack Obama was President then, and Democrats weren't trying to use the outbreak to get rid of him.

If you've ever doubted that liberals don't care about you, ponder what they did through most of 2020. Government killed small businesses. They told hair salons, nail salons, bars, restaurants, and any "non-essential" business that they couldn't open, or they put such stifling restrictions on them that many businesses couldn't open even if they were free to. And who got to decide what business was "essential?" Imagine working most of your life to build a business only to be told by some bureaucrat that it wasn't "essential." Well, it's essential to that owner—essential to pay the mortgage or the rent. In some cases, the government behaved as if America was in the Cold War Soviet Union and sent jackbooted enforcers to shut down a business. In Dallas, Texas, police were ordered to arrest a hair salon owner named Shelley Luther, who was cuffed and thrown in jail. And for what? Because she dared to open her business so she and her employees could put food on the table.

That attitude was pervasive everywhere—including Colorado. As I was out there campaigning in the thick of a pandemic, my business, Shooters Grill, was being threatened by the same draconian government mandates sweeping the rest of the country.

Make no mistake, though: there was good reason to take COVID-19 seriously. It was unknown. No one knew what was going to happen or how bad this novel illness could be. Millions of lives might be at stake.

When the local government issued its shutdown orders, I reluctantly complied. It was supposed to last just two weeks, which seems short but is a lifetime for an employee who might be living paycheck to paycheck. This would be painful, but I thought that we were all in this together, and I'd do my part to be helpful.

It wouldn't take long to realize we actually weren't all in this together. Some businesses were deemed "essential," and others, like mine, weren't. Some people got to keep their jobs. Others didn't. At Shooters, we made sure no one lost their job. It wasn't easy, but it was all Jayson and me.

Government was offering up assistance programs under the same premise that I'd already lived through during the earlier financial crisis—"It's not your fault you're shut down or hurting financially, so we, the government, will come help you." Congress set aside billions of dollars for small businesses like mine with the Payroll Protection Plan, commonly known as PPP. All I had to do was fill out the paperwork. Seemed easy enough, but as I began filling out the application, I had a sudden realization and stopped what I was doing.

I wasn't at peace about it. Some people call it intuition or conscience, but I call it the Holy Spirit. Something wasn't right.

Where were we heading with all of this? What would this look like for people, businesses, and our country once we were on the other side of this crisis? It didn't work out so well for my family and me the last time there was a national financial crisis and I tried participating in a government program. I lost my home and had my credit destroyed. There were too many unanswered questions about the PPP program. "Would the money be taxed?" "How long would it take to get it?" "Would it be enough to sustain the business?" Even if I applied and received the money, would I end up in a bureaucratic nightmare like before? Would I end up losing my business the way I'd lost my home?

Forget the PPP loan.

I focused on trying other ways to make ends meet for both me and my staff. I gathered all the employees for a meeting and told them we'd figure this out together. We talked it through to determine the things we could realistically do to survive. We came up with a few ideas, like starting delivery and curbside pickup and marketing our Shooters Grill merchandise more aggressively.

Remember when the government said "two weeks?" It wasn't. The shutdown quickly became two months. Every single day was a struggle, and we certainly weren't making ends meet. Jayson and I started using our personal savings to make payroll.

Something seemed off about the reasons for this shutdown. The data coming in about the virus didn't justify the economic toll. At that time, there'd been a total of two COVID-related deaths in all of Garfield County, and one of them was someone who'd been brought from outside the county for care. Stories were popping up from around the country about the inflated numbers—that deaths from other causes were being falsely attributed to COVID-19.

Yes, people were dying. I'm not insensitive to that. Sadly, people die every day from a lot of different things. But we don't shut down the country. An epidemic of obesity kills nearly 3 million people worldwide every year. Have we ever shut down fast-food restaurants to help prevent it? Influenza, or the flu, according to the World Health Organization, kills in the neighborhood of a quarter-million to a half-million people every year. Have we ever been ordered to shut down "non-essential" businesses for that? Nearly 3 million people die every year from alcohol consumption. Have we tried shutting down bars or liquor stores since Prohibition, or did we learn something from that?

Point is, plenty of things kill people, which is unfortunate—even one death from COVID or any of those things is one too many—but overreaching government mandates to protect people come with a cost, and that cost is your freedom. And once you give that up, you're not likely to get it back.

As we moved deeper into the pandemic, it was clear the government was choosing winners and losers. The rules didn't apply to everyone. Big-box stores were open for business. Small businesses weren't. Walmart, Target, Lowe's, Home Depot, and other big retailers had hundreds of shoppers packing their stores. Mom-and-pop stores didn't.

Later, I'd read about a restaurant owner in California whose business was shut down by the government even after she'd invested in outdoor seating so she could stay open. Meanwhile, just yards away, a movie production company set up outdoor tents to serve food to the production crew. She could only watch helplessly from the front of her now-shuttered business. For the elites of Hollywood, it was okay to operate a private catering event, but the small business owner wasn't allowed to open.

Rules for thee, but not for me. That's the liberal way.

I wondered how long would this go on and how long could my business survive?

Meanwhile, the government was getting super generous with our taxpayer money, all in the name of saving the economy, just like they had in the previous financial crisis. At the end of March 2020, I issued a campaign press release questioning why the government had agreed to send $1,200 stimulus checks to unaffected public sector employees whose jobs were never at risk. Nobody had an answer for that, and some even criticized me for pointing out the money would be far more effective if targeted solely toward those who had been actually affected through no fault of their own. Apparently, people with cushy government jobs deserved $1,200 checks, too.

In April, the Board of Commissioners of neighboring Mesa County was seeking a variance from the state to open businesses back up. Mesa County, like my own Garfield County, had very few COVID-19 cases and had a plan in place to get back open. I spoke to one of my local county commissioners, who agreed with the Mesa County plan and let me know Garfield County would soon be taking the same action with the state.

On May 4, certain small businesses, like hair salons, were permitted by the state to reopen. As if they should have ever been ordered closed in the first place. Like so many others, it had been months since I'd had a haircut. Memes were flying around the internet joking about how bad everyone's hair looked after months away from a salon. So, I was relieved when I was able to get an appointment that first day the salon reopened. Of course, there were required safety protocols, like wearing a mask. Sitting in that chair, I caught up with the latest chitchat. That's half the fun for gals at the salon.

As I sat there listening, one thing became increasingly clear—people were ticked off. They believed the government was treating small businesses unfairly. Women that weren't typically political now had plenty of opinions on how crazy things had become. Those conversations confirmed what I was already feeling—I wasn't being selfish for wanting to open back up. There were plenty of people who believed restaurants were being treated unfairly and should be allowed to reopen. I told my stylist to make sure my hair looked fabulous because I was in for the fight—I'd reopen one way or another, even if it meant another mugshot was coming my way.

I knew I had to get the doors back open.

I contacted my local county commissioner to ask how the variance for Garfield County was coming along—after all, Mesa County proved there was a responsible path forward. Restaurants there were reopening. His response floored me. He said Garfield County hadn't even submitted their variance to the state yet. He promised me weeks ago it would be submitted as soon as possible.

The more this guy talked, the worse he sounded. Here was someone I considered a friend and ally, yet he was telling me it would be another week before the commissioners would submit the variance. Then he had the nerve to tell me it wouldn't hurt me to wait.

Wow! I lit into him.

Who was he to tell me it wouldn't hurt to wait? Had he missed a paycheck? Was he forced to sit at home? No. He was going to wake up tomorrow with a job, a paycheck, and a purpose, while plenty of people were stuck at home, depressed, and powerless to do anything as their livelihoods vanished before their very eyes. I was about as pissed as I'd ever been. The lack of urgency and follow-through on his promises was appalling.

Enough was enough. I had to generate income and meet payroll, or I was going to lose my business. I decided to open my restaurant following the CDC guidelines, the same ones being used in Mesa County—they included limiting seating capacity to 30 percent, requiring the staff to wear masks, and training them on the latest sterilization and seating protocols, etc. The restrictions made it tough to sustain a business, but I'd find a way.

On May 9, 2020, I opened my restaurant in defiance of government shutdown orders.

Two days later, I met with the county commissioners and told them in no uncertain terms that they had a responsibility to get the county 100 percent open for business. I told them I'd reopened Shooters Grill a couple of days ago, and their response was that I was breaking the law, which would hinder their ability to get the variance they had yet to submit. I had to remind them of something that people in their positions should have already known—an order from the governor isn't a law. Laws are passed by the state legislature, and the governor had no right to shut down my livelihood. Besides, the commissioners were supposed to have already submitted the variance. I didn't have the luxury of waiting for them to do their jobs. I had a payroll to meet.

The next day, I sent out the following message on Twitter: "I'm not going to wait on the government to tell me what to do. The Founders never had asterisks on the Constitution. If you want freedom, you have to go out and take it."

Remember, I was a candidate for Congress, so the story made front-page news everywhere. And customers came from everywhere. Shooters was packed. People drove from hours away and waited patiently for us to serve them with our limited capacity.

My plan worked. I would be able to make payroll.

But the long arm of the law would soon be reaching out. Our local chief of police, who was generally supportive of me, hand-delivered a cease and desist letter from the county. I had to remind him that it wasn't court-ordered, so I kept Shooters open. Not long after, I was served with a court-ordered cease and desist.

Look, let's be clear. I had no interest in being a martyr for the cause. I needed to make a living, and so did the people who worked for me. I had no interest in recklessly serving people any more than I wanted to put my business at risk. The opposite was true. On a side note, if you feel unsafe patronizing a business, don't patronize it. It's called freedom of choice. To demand that a business stay closed so no one has a choice is called "tyranny."

The press was hounding me. What would this freedom-fighting restaurant owner and candidate for Congress do tomorrow? Would I voluntarily bow to the heavy hand of the government or stand firm and force their hand.

I read the court order over and over. It very clearly stated that I had to stop indoor, on-premises dining. I prayed and asked God for guidance. It felt as though everything I had worked so hard for was about to come crashing down around me. My restaurant, my campaign, and everybody who counted on me waited in the balance.

I'd made a decision.

I got some tape and cordoned off space in the public area out front. I told my staff to move the tables outside. Then I announced Shooters would remain open and serve outside, which was not prohibited by the court order.

More front-page headlines. More customers. More payroll met. More upset bureaucrats.

I explained that, once again, I was following the lead of Mesa County, where they allowed restaurants to serve their customers outside. My customers were happy, my staff was earning a living, and it was working just fine.

Rifle's chief of police, sympathetic to my cause but still having a job to do, stopped by again to let me know I couldn't occupy the city streets. If only they were so vigilant keeping city streets cleared up in, say, San Francisco. Unbelievable. At this point, how could anyone have believed keeping Shooters closed had anything to do with public health safety.

Bless his heart, the chief quickly issued Shooters a sidewalk permit, so I moved the tables from the parking area in the street to the sidewalk.

For two full days, I operated on the sidewalk with a permit.

That same week, Colorado's Governor Jared Polis went on national television with President Trump to brag about how Colorado was opening back up for business. There he was boasting about what a fine job he was doing on behalf of the people of Colorado. Except it wasn't true. Not for restaurant owners like me, anyway. Truth be told, it was going to get worse.

A county commissioner came over to scold me, saying I was putting everything at risk for the county. The commission was afraid the state would take over all municipal functions if I didn't toe the line. Then on Friday, May 15, the public health department revoked my license to serve food.

The government bureaucrats got me. They shut me down. I wasn't going to operate without a license and break the law. There's no getting around that.

Then a curious thing happened. Customers started taping money to the front door of the restaurant to show their support. Since the tables were still out on the sidewalk, people held private picnics outside, complete with American flags waving. A neighboring business opened a GoFundMe account, which would eventually raise $6,000 that I gave to my staff.

The health department dragged its feet with my license, while the rest of Garfield County opened for business. I called a lawyer to work with the county attorney to resolve the issue. It was relayed to me that the health department didn't like how I had skirted the intention of their rules.

See, this had nothing to do with health; it was all about power.

Eventually, the health department reinstated our license, and Shooters was again open for business. The city of Rifle was helpful in putting seating platforms in the parking lots of many local businesses so that restaurants like Shooters could serve their customers outside.

Finally, an example of how the government should work. It should seek solutions by collaborating with private citizens to find a way forward—instead of forcing people to live under their authoritarian rules. Government should take a balanced approach in handling a crisis. You don't just start selectively closing businesses and doling out money to anyone who asks. Determine the most vulnerable among us who were negatively affected through no fault of their own and help them.

A year and a half after the pandemic began, the government was still paying many people more in unemployment benefits than they would otherwise be earning at a job. It's no wonder so many people didn't bother looking for work. Those benefits ended in September 2021— and thank goodness they did. That sort of spending isn't sustainable and hurts the economy. Besides, many small businesses that did try to reopen couldn't because there was a shortage of workers due to the enhanced unemployment benefits.

A small business owner can't really compete with the government for employees. One coffee shop in a small town where I'd been campaigning had a sign on the front door that said they'd open as soon as anyone would accept twenty dollars an hour to come work for them, no experience required. A lot of people supported this type of government assistance, not realizing that over the long term, it'll break the backbone of our small business economy.

President Trump often said we can't have the cure be worse than this disease. I agree.

There's an untold number of terrible outcomes from this pandemic, many of which were self-inflicted. Former New York governor, Andrew Cuomo, forcing elderly COVID-19 patients into nursing homes, which eventually led to their deaths, certainly comes to mind. Out-of-control spending and inflation make the list. I also worry about the long-term consequences for an entire generation of children living in cocooned safe spaces designed to protect them from a virus they're not at high risk of dying from.

The pandemic reinforced my notion that our rugged individualism and desire to be free should trump the heavy hand of government.

In a free society, the government steps aside to allow adults to make informed decisions for themselves. Never trust politicians who wield their authority in ways contrary to the authority granted by We the People. Never again should the government be allowed to infringe on the rights afforded us by the Constitution of the United States of America.

Through the whole of 2020, as I battled to reopen Shooters and win the job representing the 3rd Congressional District, I'd grown more determined than ever to fight to preserve our country.

And now that I'd won a seat in Congress, I was off to do just that.

★　★　★

MRS. BOEBERT
GOES TO
WASHINGTON

★　★　★

CHAPTER 25

Who Really Wants
to Compromise?

A merica faces a lot of challenges—illegal immigration, the national debt, gun rights, freedom of speech, entitlement reform, criminal justice reform, and school choice, to name a few. Who's tackling them? Certainly not Washington. Democrats have so succeeded in party polarization and fostering divisiveness that there's no more "reaching across the aisle." Nothing gets done because no one works together.

On the campaign trail, I took criticism because I held the position that Republicans shouldn't compromise in giving Democrats what they want today in the hopes they'll return the favor in the future. After all, as history shows, they never hold up their end of the bargain. What do Democrats ever concede to Republicans?

The primary example I gave was President Ronald Reagan's 1986 Immigration Reform and Control Act, which immediately gave amnesty to 3 million or so illegal immigrants but failed to actually control illegal immigration. My comments were then taken by Mitsch Bush and turned into a multi-million-dollar attack ad campaign, saying I'd be too rigid and unwilling to compromise as a member of Congress.

I just had to laugh when I saw that ad.

For one thing, I never said I was against compromise. Far from it. I was simply saying conservatives shouldn't punt on what they're fighting for on the false hope that someday the Democrats would agree to give us something back. Compromise should be about both sides getting some of what they want. It doesn't mean one party gets everything they want and the other gets nothing.

In recent memory, it seems conservatives have compromised on a lot of issues and gotten nothing in return. Is there a genuine need to rack up the national debt? Let's talk about a balanced budget amendment. If you believe there's a need for more education dollars? Let's talk about expanding school choice. Want mail-in voting? What are you going to do to put in protections to ensure only legal votes are counted? Well, on that last one, forget it. Democrats have already fought against that. We saw it in 2021 when Texas Democrats fought against their state's voting integrity bill, which would later be passed by the state's Republican majority. If a Democrat agreed to mail-in voting protections, they'd have to say "goodbye" to ballot harvesting and the votes they get from dead people and illegal aliens.

The second thing about that attack and accusing me of being unwilling to compromise was that I knew my conservative supporters understood exactly what I was saying. I'd often get messages encouraging me to stay the course. My supporters are a lot like me—tired of caving to the insatiable demands of the Left.

While researching for this book, I came across a poll conducted a few years ago by *The Economist* that asked whether people would prefer having a member of Congress who was willing to compromise or stick to their principles no matter what. The results showed nearly 90 percent of Democrats would sell out their principles, and for Independents, the figure was just more than 70 percent. For the Republicans surveyed, it was about a 50/50 split.

I disagree with the premise of the question because I don't think the two are mutually exclusive. I think you can stand up for your principles *and* be willing to compromise. I'm certainly open to compromise—but it doesn't mean I'm selling out my principles. I do still think the poll results shed some light on a fundamental difference between the two parties and help explain why our approach is so different for so many of the problems facing the country.

Democrats often own the emotional argument and fail at getting the policy right. Republicans often own the right policy and lose the emotional argument. It's like a political version of the bestselling relationship book, *Men Are from Mars, Women Are from Venus*. We're talking different languages, which makes finding common ground difficult.

Look, I have to say the Democrats have done an outstanding job of owning the emotions of our nation's political policies. It's reflected in that poll. They've framed public policy arguments in such a way that makes Republicans seem mean, insensitive, even cruel, while they seem caring and compassionate. "Health care is a right!" they'll say. "How can we afford to cut funding for grandma?" "Those poor Dreamers. They deserve a chance! Give them a free college education!" We'll just have to pretend not to know Dreamers are here because of a failed immigration policy.

Democrats will even blame Republicans for things Democrats did. Remember the images of illegal immigrant kids at the border? "Oh my God, Trump has them in cages!" Democrats won't tell you those pictures were taken when Obama was President, as part of a program instituted by his administration.

So, it's no surprise Democrats, with help from their friends in the mainstream national news media, are portrayed as more caring than Republicans. They pretend to support the idea of compromise, because, by definition, compromise means you're willing to be reasonable, thoughtful, and caring, unlike those uncaring and rigid Republicans.

The irony is that Democrats are almost never willing to compromise. This is something President Trump exposed time and again. Want to do a deal on infrastructure, DACA, stimulus? No, no, and no. Nancy Pelosi wanted to impeach him instead.

The President offered deals that sometimes conservatives didn't like, but even then, Democrats wouldn't compromise and take those deals because they might make President Trump look good. On the flip side, look at how Obamacare passed without a single Republican vote. That very, very expensive program affects a huge part of our economy, was opposed by the entire Republican party, yet Democrats passed it anyway. Compromise, anyone?

Before I'd been sworn in as a United States representative, I gave considerable thought to how I'd determine which way I'd vote on an issue. Am I willing to compromise? Absolutely. Do I stay true to what I said on the campaign trail? Absolutely. Will I agree to legislation that offers Democrats what I oppose in exchange for hoping they'll agree with me sometime later? Absolutely not.

Take immigration reform, for example. More than 80 percent of Americans believe the immigration system needs major reforms. It seems like an issue ripe for compromise. I've said I'm open to legal immigration reform, but my red line is that such legislation must include building the wall and securing the border first. Without that, any talk of immigration reform simply becomes leverage for amnesty and more illegal activity.

Securing the border first seems like a reasonable position to take, but the Democrats are having none of it. Since Joe Biden took office as President, Texas has been inundated with millions of people illegally pouring in through the border, and Democrats refuse to do anything about it because they support open borders. Texas Governor Greg Abbott decided the state would build the wall itself, and he dispatched law enforcement officers to do what Biden wouldn't. Democrats have made it clear they will not compromise their position on illegal immigration. Why would they? Democrats hope illegal immigrants turn Texas blue, and by granting them amnesty, they hope to create a whole new voting bloc.

Democrats are also very good at virtue signaling. They make the case that it's mean and morally wrong to make these people go through the legal channels to enter the United States. But securing the border isn't mean; it's moral. That's where Republicans need to step up and make a better argument for securing the border. Among other things, securing the border reduces drug and sex trafficking and prevents waves of criminals from entering the country. Those issues alone ought to be enough to want secure borders.

We should also be better about messaging on how generous our country is. The United States is, by far, the biggest net recipient of immigrants worldwide, legal or illegal, totaling 59 million people between 1965 and 2015. This influx accounted for 55 percent of the nation's population growth during that period. It's not unreasonable to suggest that an influx like that is going to cost a whole lot of money.

Republicans can do a better job at making the argument that it's immoral to promote open borders, call for eliminating ICE, and allow sanctuary cities.

These policies are like a vacuum, pulling people in from everywhere without them going through the legal process. They create an incentive for people to cross the border illegally, who now know nothing will be done about it. Why wouldn't someone from a third-world country try to come here? Democrats will give them free education and free health care. And as a bonus, if they have a child born here, the child will automatically be an American citizen, even if their mother entered America illegally.

Democrats have sent the world the message that it's okay to break our immigration laws; they'll protect anyone who dares cross. That message encourages dangerous behavior that puts our law enforcement officers at risk, strains our social services, and creates unsustainable financial challenges for local, state, and federal governments. Democrats rarely, if ever, put Americans first.

But if you oppose such behavior, you'll be attacked by Democrats and their propaganda arm, the mainstream media.

We've all heard the Democrats' arguments: Children of illegal immigrants are here through no fault of their own. They need schooling, health care, and education. Our businesses need these people to pick our crops, clean our houses, etc. My answer to that is I want an immigration system that works. I want a system that takes away the incentives to come here illegally. Our immigration system needs to be merit-based, such that the people who are allowed to come here have the skills needed to fill jobs Americans either can't or won't fill. I want a system that's safe and secure for all involved. We also need more than just a viable entry system; we also need a viable *exit* system—one that ensures people who were only approved for temporary stays leave when they're supposed to.

There are plenty of ways to compromise to get to an immigration system that works, even on points usually resisted by Republicans. The rule of law cannot be compromised. We need to enforce the immigration laws we already have on the books. We need to address the fundamental incentives encouraging illegal behavior. That starts with securing the border. Also, it's time we boot out the illegal, hardened criminals with a big, swift kick. It's the moral thing to do.

Beyond immigration and in the bigger scheme of things, too often, Republicans cave when Democrats make them look like the bad guys. My fellow Republicans, the Democrat argument for illegal immigration is not a moral one! It's time we stick up for our core principles first and then negotiate on the details. But too often, we don't.

Why is it that even when Republicans control all three branches of government, they fail to deliver on reducing the debt, balancing the budget, entitlement reform, or term limits, to name a few? The common-sense answer is fear of negative perception and the consequences that come with that. Seems we're always worried about the next election.

As this book went to press, the United States is $28 trillion in debt. Now, it's likely trillions more. We have a record number of illegal immigrants and Democrats pushing policies once thought unconscionable—defunding the police and socialized medicine. Why? Too often, we set aside our core principles to appease the mob, and we end up with policies that make no sense. Our behavior doesn't win Republicans votes. It just emboldens Democrats to push their policies further to the left.

Forget what the coastal elitists try to get you to believe. I believe we're generally a conservative nation. Most people want reasonable solutions—for every issue.

The environment? I come from the west, where the great outdoors isn't just a vacation idea but a way of life. The Republicans I know here care deeply about clean air and water and are committed to protecting our natural resources.

Minimum wage? The Republican business owners I know want to take good care of their employees, and they want the freedom to pay their employees a fair wage and benefits without being ordered by the government what that wage has to be.

Energy? The Republican energy workers I know want to produce energy responsibly, take good care of the land they're using to do that, and provide high-paying jobs right here in the United States.

Natural Resources? The Republican outdoorsmen I know want access to hunt, ride their horses and ATVs, fish, and camp in the forests, covering thousands of acres in my district, without polluting or damaging the land they care so deeply for.

From my perspective, Republicans are often very good on the issues we get criticized for. We should campaign more on why we believe in what we believe and worry less about the attacks that will inevitably come from the Democrats and their friends in the media. We should work on legislation that focuses on solving problems, hopefully on common ground with reasonably-minded Democrats. If there is no common ground, we should win on the merits of our ideas or find candidates who can make the case.

We must ask the hard questions. "Can we afford it?" "Does it promote freedom?" "Is it in the best interests of our country?" "Is it Constitutional?" I'm not convinced we ask these basic questions often enough, but they can help guide us to the right answer.

Finally, we need to remember that people vote based on how they want to be represented. They get frustrated when they elect someone to do a job and then that person votes differently once they get to DC. My voting record reflects my conservative principles. People elected me to vote a certain way, and I honor that.

Voters expect me to oppose policies that are bad for the country, things like the Green New Deal and Medicare for All.

Here's the thing, though. For any issue, there's a workable solution. The expansion of cleaner energy around the globe? Expand the markets for American-produced clean coal and natural gas, because they're cleaner than what's used now in many countries. Affordable health care? There's a workable solution. Allow competition, price transparency, and portability to help drive better outcomes at lower prices.

Collectively, in Congress, we've got to focus on solving problems. As a Republican representative, I'll be happy to compromise and find common ground, as long as we don't compromise our core conservative principles.

★ ★ ★ CHAPTER 26 ★ ★ ★

How about a Personal Option for Education and Health Care?

One of the reasons I ran for Congress, and you'll hear me say this a lot, is I don't want my four sons to grow up in a socialist country. Every time I faced a challenge on the campaign trail or another negative story, all I thought about was Tyler, Brody, Kaydon, and Roman, and I kept fighting.

I encourage each of them to study hard because, despite what anyone might think, I believe in the value of education. Yes, I regrettably dropped out of high school—to work and help Mom put food on the table—but it doesn't alter my opinion that American children should receive the highest quality education available anywhere in the world. Most parents want the same thing for their kids. But America's current system makes that near impossible unless we fight for better alternatives—which is exactly what I decided to do when I got to Washington.

The United States spends an average of $12,612 per student per year on public schools. In New York, public schools spend twice that at

$24,040 per student, and the federal government contributes $1,200 of that. In Colorado, the spend is half of New York's at $10,020 per student, with the feds kicking in $780.

That's a lot of your money being spent on school systems not every parent is happy with. Some schools now teach critical race theory, others, sex education, and still others employ teachers who push their politics on their students. If these aren't the sorts of things you want to be taught to your kids, shouldn't you have the choice to send them elsewhere and have that education money spent there instead?

What about health care? Shouldn't you have the right to choose where the health-care dollars allocated to you from your employer is spent?

I've yet to meet anyone who says that our public schools or our health-care system are delivering the best outcomes for the best price available for everyone who pays for these services. Instead, we get rising costs and worse outcomes. The last time I checked, education and health insurance costs have skyrocketed, leaving many families buried in debt.

Sure, liberals are pro-choice if it allows women to kill their own babies, but they aren't pro-choice on education and certainly aren't pro-choice on anything else in health care. Instead of embracing the freedom of choice that adults make their own decisions, liberals consistently cling to big government solutions.

Let's remember: Democrats got everything they wanted when they passed the Affordable Care Act without a single Republican vote. They promised the ACA would make health care more affordable (hence the name) and that you'd be able to keep your doctors. Lies. Now they expect us to go along with their scheme to spend another $30–40 trillion on the Medicare for All socialized medicine scheme.

If big government solutions worked so well, you'd think our K-12 public schools would be killing it. The public education system is almost exclusively controlled by Democrat-run teachers' unions and funded by taxpayers. These are the same unions that always fight school choice and charter schools and never think there's enough money being spent on education at any level. Once again, the Democrats are anti-choice.

It's the same problem with higher education. How many of our tax dollars have gone toward subsidizing tenured liberal professors who indoctrinate our children with wild notions about the nobility of socialism and communism? We fund that sort of thing when the money could be better spent on trade schools that teach usable, real-world skills.

The government is complicit in all this madness. In the race to get more kids to enroll in traditional colleges, the government allowed easy access to student loans that, surprise, many people can't afford to pay back. The easy money fueled a surge in enrollment and a huge spike in the cost of tuition. Democrats never understand simple economics. Colleges can raise their tuition because they know student loans will cover the costs. When the students become young adults and then complain about the debt they can't pay, Democrats call for "wiping out" student loan debt as if "poof" the wave of a magic wand will make it disappear. Economics doesn't work that way—the debt doesn't just vanish, someone still has to pay it, and that someone is you.

Liberals never seem to understand that those who ignore history are doomed to repeat it. This student loan fiasco feels, in a lot of ways, like a new version of the subprime mortgage disaster of 2008. Hold onto your hats—and wallets.

The Democrats' solution to this mess isn't to force colleges with multi-billion-dollar endowments to stop accepting student loans, temper pay increases for tenured professors, or stop paying for country club memberships for university leadership. Nope. Their solution is to "wipe out" the student loan debt and offer a "tuition free" college education. Once again, someone has to pay for this, and that someone, as always, is you.

In health care, it's the same sort of thing. Democrats want a public option—where the government basically runs health care. Imagine sitting at the doctors' office feeling like you're at the DMV. That's what would happen. Democrats want true socialized medicine and will cite the greatness of government-run health care in places like England. Yes, socialized health care across the pond is so great that care is rationed, millions wait in a queue to see a doctor, and thousands have died because they couldn't get treatment in time. Oh, did I mention they also have a shortage of doctors and nurses?

Is that what we really want for America? I certainly don't.

I suggest we take a step back and consider the big picture. It'd be wise to look outside of the health-care industry and study the success of companies like Uber, Amazon, Netflix, and Airbnb. These companies disrupted transportation, shopping, entertainment, and travel by bypassing the middleman and enabling the service provider and the customer to work together directly. There's efficiency in that. Can we apply those same principles to health care?

Someone who needs a ride can still hail a cab—keep in mind, taxicab companies often have a monopoly on passenger transportation. In some cities, government regulation keeps out competitors. Or you can call Uber.

You have a choice.

Look at Netflix. They've not told anyone to stop going to the movie theater. They don't have to. Netflix offers entertainment options, and the consumer can choose for themselves what works best for them.

Uber, Amazon, Netflix, and Airbnb are just a few examples showing consumers have options. These companies are successful because they allowed the free market to work and offered services that make life easier—and often less expensive—for a lot of people. Nevertheless, if you don't want to patronize any of these companies, that's okay. You can still call a taxi, shop in a store, go to a movie theater, and stay in a hotel. The point is you have a choice.

Shouldn't health care operate the same way?

Every solution I hear from Democrats is more government control and more government spending, be it on health care or education.

So, what should Republicans do?

First, let's make it clear we intend to keep the promises we made to the American people. Don't spend a decade saying you're going to repeal and replace Obamacare and then not do it. Look, I have no interest in taking away anyone's health insurance. I don't want to prevent people from being able to receive treatment for preexisting conditions, and I certainly have no desire to end lunch programs for kids. But moving forward, Republicans have to keep their promises when they make new ones.

Let's not waste our time fighting powerful public teachers' unions, even though they're failures. It's also not a winning strategy to fund the Department of Education or to push for national standards or horrible programs like No Child Left Behind. "Democrat-lite" isn't my cup of tea.

We should focus our time, effort, and energy on providing more free-market choices. Where Democrats push for public options, Republicans should offer personal options. These won't remove anything from an existing program, but they will empower individuals to take control of their own health care and education spending. I think it's worth a shot and is what personal freedom is all about.

Let me lay it out for you.

Personal Option for Education

I'm the poster child for how one-size-fits-all public education doesn't work for everyone. I can't say the government made good use of the money they were spending on fifteen-year-old me. At that time, I was more concerned with helping put food on our family's table than I was with school. The idea of going to college was also out of touch with my reality.

Regardless of your education path, you should have a choice in the matter. Maybe that path looks like a traditional public school. Maybe it doesn't. Maybe it looks like college. Maybe it means learning a trade or coding. Maybe it's beauty or nursing school. Maybe you don't know right now.

The United States of America spends an average of $12,000 per student per year on your K-12 education. What if you could opt out of that public education spend and have that money deposited into an education savings account, then given the choice as to how you spend it on your education?

Would some students be better served by having schools compete for their "business?" Would some teachers be more entrepreneurial if given the opportunity to compete for students? Would choices, options, and outcomes improve by empowering individuals to make these decisions themselves instead of having them decided based merely on their zip code?

I think so. If you disagree with the choices, that's okay too. You can keep going to the public school just as you do now.

States that want to pursue a personal option for education should do so. They should build a framework that works best for their needs, not one prescribed for them by the federal government. In Washington, DC, we should make sure the bureaucracy gets out of the way of the states who want to pursue this.

My challenge to you is this—get your local school board or your state board of education, or your governor to push for a personal option for education. Who knows? Maybe you'll be the one that launches the "Uber" for your kids' education. I believe as people take more control of their futures, we'll see more innovation, efficiency, and better outcomes.

I'll be happy to do my part to help get the federal government out of your way.

Personal Option for Health Care

More than 150 million Americans get their health insurance from their employer, and most of them are happy with it, so I don't want to tinker with that. That said, I've never met a business owner who wants to be the middleman choosing their employees' health-care options. We should give those businesses more flexibility to simply fund personal health-care accounts.

Imagine your company's next health insurance enrollment period, where they're offering health plans that they've pre-selected to fund for you. But this time, they'll let you opt out—they'll take the money they'd spend on the policy and instead deposit it into a health spending account. It would be an HSA on steroids—money in an account you can use on your health care as you see fit. If your employer funds it, great. If you want to add to it yourself, great. If someone else wants to help fund it, great. This would be your account that stays with you forever, from the time you're born until the day you die. And after that, you can pass it along to others as you see fit.

Most of us manage to buy our own car insurance. I think we can handle the same for health care. You should be able to decide what insurance works best for you and buy it directly.

I'd imagine a great number of employees would continue using the health insurance the company provides. But I believe there are also a number of people who would like to make that decision for themselves.

As a bonus, the flexibility of this plan would make it more affordable for smaller businesses to provide a health insurance benefit. At Shooters, which is a fairly small restaurant, we can't afford to buy health-care plans for our staff. So, it would be nice to have an option to fund an employee's personal health account at a rate that I, as the business owner, determined we could afford.

What the option does is help make the system portable. Instead of being stuck to your employer because of the health insurance they offer, the personal health account would travel with you. You own it and control how the money is spent. You become a shopper for health care. Insurance companies would compete for your business. Health-care providers would compete for your health-care dollars. Now we've provided a direct relationship between you, providers, and insurance companies. For a rural district like mine, this could incentivize large insurance companies to compete for business from our citizens, people who are largely ignored in favor of large employers and urban centers.

Congressional Republicans are already doing some innovative work on this. Representative Chip Roy from Texas has proposed legislation for Health Freedom Accounts, which, as I've outlined, would empower people to take control of their health spending.

Unfortunately, this innovative messaging is drowned out every time Republicans try to repeal or replace existing programs. How many times has the press criticized Republicans for not offering an alternative solution even though Republicans do have solid proposals? We should think more like Uber, Amazon, Netflix, and Airbnb. Bypass the existing system. Let's unify around innovation. Get Washington, DC, out of the way.

If we give employers and individuals more options, we might be able to help chip away at the $800 billion Americans spend on administrative costs. That way, doctors can spend more time on patient care and less time dealing with insurance companies or the government.

My second challenge is for big businesses to get on board and demonstrate how effective a private option for health care can be. Let's start by testing this with the very companies I've mentioned here—Uber, Amazon, Netflix, and Airbnb. You've changed business in America by empowering individuals with choices. Help do the same for their health care by giving your employees a choice and let's see how it goes.

I'll do my part in Washington, DC, to help get the regulatory burdens out of the way.

The personal options for education and health care are not solutions for everyone. But they can make a big difference. They don't require us to dismantle existing programs. They don't require bills so long we can't even read them before they become laws. Personal options for education and health care do require the will of people who want more personal freedom in these important areas of their lives—and that's something worth pursuing.

CHAPTER 27

Meeting President Trump

By the time I'd arrived in Washington, DC, I'd become struck with the enormity of what had happened to me and my family. Less than a year earlier, I'd seen the Capitol for the first time as a tourist, and now here I was as an actual member of the United States House of Representatives. Let me tell you, if you fight hard enough, dreams absolutely do come true in America.

After I'd won the Republican primary against Scott Tipton, remember President Trump had called to say he was looking forward to having a fighter join him in Washington. Well, here I was!

I was on the Trump Train long before I even considered running for public office. President Trump represented everything I felt an effective President should be. He was an outsider, wasn't trying to fit in, worked to "drain the swamp," and, both domestically and internationally, put America first. He was also the first politician that spoke in a language I could truly relate to.

The irony that a billionaire businessman could relate to everyday folks from blue-collar backgrounds wasn't lost on me. President Trump grew up on construction sites, working with New York's union construction crews. That sort of thing goes a long way toward learning how to relate with regular folk. His slogan "Make America Great Again" is something millions of working-class people embraced because they're the ones affected most by things like illegal immigration and policies that put their jobs in jeopardy.

President Trump was a lot like that new boss who comes into a failing business and vows changes to turn its fortunes around. Then legacy employees who live by the mantra, "But we've always done it this way," whine and complain when the new boss shakes up the status quo. That's how it was for President Trump. America was failing on many fronts, and the entrenched, liberal career-politicians who created the mess knew their day had come. So, from the very day he came down the escalator at Trump Tower to announce his candidacy, President Trump was a target of the Left. The irony is that the liberals accused him of being "mean." "Oh, look at his mean tweets!" they'd cry. But those tweets weren't nearly as "mean" as the Left's dishonest attacks.

People like me never saw President Trump as mean. We felt the exact opposite—and still do. We saw a man standing up for those who'd felt ignored by the ruling class. Here was a guy looking out for us. Was President Trump perfect? No. But who among us is?

You can never overstate the sheer thrill and excitement of receiving a phone call from the President of the United States. You just can't put into words what it's like. The phone rings, you pick it up, and a voice says, "Please hold for the President, Ms. Boebert." I was Lauren Boebert of Rifle, Colorado. Heck, it wasn't that long ago that I was working at the drive-thru at a McDonald's. Now, the most powerful human being in the free world was on the other end of the phone, wanting to talk with me. Can you imagine? The President told me he'd been following my campaign and expressed concern that my opponent in the general election, Diane Mitsch Bush, had built a good-sized campaign war chest. He knew she could outspend me. My answer was that I was a small business owner and the mother of four boys, so I knew how to stretch a dime into a dollar. He said that was "fantastic" and even called me a "dynamo."

The conversation shifted to my carrying a gun and the importance of the Second Amendment. Somehow, I found the brass to tell him he hadn't done the best job of defending our gun rights and encouraged him to never allow them to be taken away. Seriously. I'd just gently chided the President of the United States. I guess I really was a "dynamo."

We chatted a bit about the idiocy of the movement in Seattle, where anarchists took over six downtown city blocks and created the Capitol Hill Autonomous Zone (CHAZ). These leftist lunatics were demanding, among other things, that Seattle cut its budget for police in half. I was, and still am, very much against any effort to defund the police. The President took a stand and told me how he'd made it clear to Seattle's civic leaders that he'd send in the National Guard if they didn't get their city back under control. Once they got the message, they closed up CHAZ.

In any case, we exchanged some banter about our families, and to my great surprise, President Trump extended an invitation to meet the first lady and him at Mt. Rushmore for his upcoming rally and patriotic celebration the day before Independence Day. I'd already planned to attend that rally, but wow, to now have the chance to meet both him and Melania face-to-face? I was very happy to accept his invitation.

Before we'd hung up, I thanked President Trump for the sacrifice he'd made for so many of us. He shared a bit about how he'd had a nice life, but since becoming President, he had been forced to battle the maniacs from the Left every day. Now that I'm in Congress, I know exactly what he's talking about.

After that call, my heart was racing! The President of the United States had called me! Before hanging up, he let me know that both he and House Minority Leader Kevin McCarthy would be supporting my campaign.

It was beautiful.

Weeks later, Jayson and I brought the boys up to Mt. Rushmore for the celebration of America. I'd never been there before, and let me tell you, the pictures don't do it justice. What an incredible place. Not only was I caught off guard by the beauty of the Black Hills of South Dakota, but also by the sheer number of people who were now reaching out to help me navigate the unchartered waters of a general election campaign.

Representative Mark Wayne Mullin from Oklahoma invited me to join him and Missouri Representative Jason Smith for a meeting at the home of South Dakota Governor Kristi Noem. She's one of my favorite conservatives and someone I look up to as a role model. When we met, she and her family could not have been more welcoming to my family and me.

What we all thought would be about a fifteen-minute meeting turned into an hour-long conversation in the backyard. The governor gave me some great advice about how to navigate the day-to-day challenges I'd face in Congress—things like how to make effective use of my time, how to keep my priorities straight, and how to accomplish what I wanted to without neglecting time with my family. She was the perfect messenger because before she became South Dakota's first-ever female governor, Noem had also been a member of Congress and a mom with young kids. Somehow, she found a way to balance all of that with an eight-hour commute to work in DC.

The governor's husband, Bryon, shared with Jayson some of the challenges of being married to a high-profile elected official. All in all, it was a warm, gracious, and informative meeting that reinforced my admiration of Governor Noem. She's classy, down-to-earth, and truly loves her family, her state, and her country.

Later that day, my family and I headed over to the base of Mt. Rushmore for the big event. It was a perfect afternoon, and the atmosphere was electric. I couldn't believe Jayson and I were just hours away from meeting the President of the United States.

Before President Trump would arrive, the Secret Service went through its paces in preparing the security. As with the other VIP guests, Jayson and I were sent backstage to take a COVID-19 test and held in a room for four hours. While we were waiting, I felt something tickling my leg and looked down to find a thread dangling from my dress. I was afraid to pull at it because, who knows, the entire hem might have unraveled before I met the President! That's when what I like to call my "Rifle redneck instinct" kicked in. There were no safety pins to be found, and as I passed by a desk, I noticed a stapler and had a "eureka" moment. I grabbed the stapler and went to work fixing the hem. All Jayson could do was shake his head and start snapping pictures. I said, "Hey, it works." I posted a picture on social media, and thousands agreed I did what needed to be done.

With the hem of my dress now firmly in place, Representative Dusty Johnson, who serves South Dakota's at-large district, visited with us for a few minutes. He's one of those people who's easy to take a quick liking to. Johnson has a dry sense of humor and a quick wit, and we made an instant connection. It's easy to see why he's so popular in South Dakota. Our chat reminded me of the importance of first impressions and kindness, especially in politics.

When the first family of South Dakota arrived, Governor Noem's husband greeted Jayson, then pointed at me and asked, "I'm sorry, who are you again?" These were definitely my kind of people.

We watched Air Force One, then Marine One, fly over against the backdrop of Mt. Rushmore. The time to meet the President and first lady was fast approaching. Sarah Huckabee Sanders and her family were on the schedule to meet President Trump first, followed by Jayson and me. Sarah couldn't have been any kinder, and it was fun to see her wearing her "mom" hat. Sarah's kids were having a great time laughing and playing, and it was clear she had a loving family. It made me think about the balancing act she likely had to do between working as a fantastic press secretary and as a mom. She clearly did a great job on both fronts.

Now the moment had arrived for us to meet President Trump and Melania. This can be a bit of a nerve-racking experience for anyone. I don't know what was going through Jayson's mind, but you could see it in his face—he knew it wasn't going to be like saying "Hey" to the guys on the gas rigs.

Initially, we thought this would be nothing more than a quick photo op, but it was so much more. When I approached him, Jayson and I introduced ourselves, and the President turned to the first lady and said, "Melania, this is the girl I was telling you about. The one who won by 10 points. The one who carries a gun in her restaurant. Lauren, real guns? (I nodded) Real guns, Melania."

Holy smokes!

So, there we were with the President and first lady. If you've not seen Melania Trump in person, you might not know just how beautiful she is. She had, after all, been a successful model. But Melania's beauty wasn't just outward but inward, too. She's one of the kindest people I've ever met. At that moment, I felt compelled to shake Melania's hand but then remembered that it was a "no-no" because of the COVID-19 safety protocols. I imagined the Secret Service tasering me for that faux pas. Glad they didn't, although they might have saved me the embarrassment of that handshake—one of the most awkward ever. As I reached in, I made everything worse by pulling my hand back away. Not my smoothest move. Nevertheless, Melania was quite gracious.

We were supposed to head to our seats after meeting the President, but why stop with him? As Governor Noem was presenting President Trump with a special bust of Mt. Rushmore that included his face alongside Roosevelt, Lincoln, Washington, and Jefferson, I made my way over to Secretary of the Interior David Bernhardt. I introduced myself, knowing that he, too, was from Rifle. After Governor Noem wrapped up her presentation, President Trump and Melania, along with Kevin McCarthy, came over to again congratulate me on my primary victory. The President told McCarthy how proud he was of me and to make sure I got all of the support I needed.

Now we were ready to take our seats. I caught Eric and Lara Trump out of the corner of my eye. It wasn't hard—they're tall and stand out, big time. I asked for a picture, and we chatted about Colorado, my race, and the Second Amendment. Eric said he was a big fan of my Shooters Grill "God, Guns, Trump" hat. He'd later be very supportive during our general election campaign. I was grateful for the opportunity to meet both him and his beautiful wife.

Now, finally, Jayson and I were going to our seats. But before we did, I stood there on the stage and soaked it all in. The stage was three-tiered, covered in red, white, and blue, with fourteen American flags adorning the wall behind the President's podium. A military band sat on the first tier in front, with VIPs seated on both the right and left sides of the stage. With the band playing in the background, I looked at my family, sitting in the audience and awaiting the President to speak, and was overcome with emotion. The patriotism on display here warmed my heart, and along with having just met the President of the United States, it reinforced how important it was that I do everything I could to help Make America Great Again.

Four months later, I won the election.

★　　★　　★　CHAPTER 28　★　　★　　★

The Oval Office

T hough I had won my race, the 2020 election was bittersweet. On one hand, I was now an elected member of Congress, which was amazing. But on the other hand, I wouldn't be able to celebrate with the President. Joe Biden was now the President-elect after an election victory that looked spurious at best. President Trump's team was now engaged in legal challenges in various states over the election results.

As the controversy over the results swirled throughout the country and the beltway, I followed up on a request I'd made earlier in my campaign to White House Chief of Staff, Mark Meadows. I'd asked for the opportunity to meet with President Trump the next time I was in Washington DC, and well, now I was here. Meadows arranged for three of us newly elected freshmen representatives to come to the Oval Office and meet with the President.

When we arrived, the President was running late. We'd been waiting in the West Wing for about twenty minutes when a staff member came to take us to the Oval Office. The only time I'd ever seen the West Wing before was on television shows. Obviously, those were sets on a soundstage and always looked pretty good-sized, but in reality, the West Wing is much smaller than it appears on TV. The hallways are tight and bustling with activity.

This was some morning: I was actually inside the White House! I tried to focus, but the two sides of my brain were fighting each other. One tried to stay rational, but the other was in awe of being in the White House and on the way to meet the President in the Oval Office.

There really aren't words to describe how surreal the feeling is of stepping into the Oval Office for the first time. There he was, the President of the United States, talking on the phone while sitting behind the Resolute desk. Over to the side were Meadows and Kaleigh McEnany, the President's press secretary—and me! What a wonderful mix of emotions—pride, patriotism, humility, awe—washing over me. How did I get here? Everything was suddenly big and overwhelming in a beautiful way.

President Trump welcomed us as he was on his conference call and told whoever was on the other end of the line that he'd invited a few freshman members of Congress to join him. I stood dead center in front of the Resolute desk and said a brief, "Hello." The conference call went on for another fifteen minutes, and the President had a little fun with us along the way. After the call wrapped up, he congratulated each of us on our victories. When President Trump spoke to me, he wore a big smile. He was still amazed by Shooters Grill, the place where the girls carry real guns while they work.

Though the President was welcoming, cordial, and seemingly happy, you could tell the weight of his own election issues was undoubtedly present. The conversation with our group lasted around forty minutes, and then the President gave us a quick tour of the Oval Office. As he did, I told him that part of my faith is that believers will lay hands on people for good blessings. So, I placed my hand on his arm and said a short prayer as he closed his eyes and nodded. He was more than gracious throughout our visit and was kind enough to allow me to get a picture with him behind his desk.

It was a moment I will never forget.

Before leaving, I thanked the President of the United States again for everything he'd done for the country and for taking the time to meet with me.

Then I was on my way.

★ ★ ★ CHAPTER 29 ★ ★ ★

Challenging the Results

I left that Oval Office meeting overcome with emotion. I couldn't believe that had just happened. In barely more than a year, I went from sitting in the kitchen with Jayson, discussing whether to run for office, to sitting in the Oval Office.

Only in America.

Though I was excited about my meeting with President Trump, I also felt sad, not just that he'd lost his bid for reelection, but that something with the election itself didn't seem right. States run by Democrats had used the pandemic as an excuse to bypass the rules of the Constitution and institute mail-in voting without the approval of their state legislatures.

So, a month later, three days after I took my oath of office, I joined 146 Republican members of Congress and challenged the Electoral College certification of the 2020 Presidential election. Contrary to what the Left has repeatedly said, we weren't trying to overturn the election that day. We simply believed the United States Congress needed to independently gather the facts, debate, then make an informed decision before certifying the election.

Democrats seem to forget, or they just don't want you to know, that four years earlier, several Democrats in the House challenged President Trump's Electoral College victory. Representative Sheila Jackson Lee from Texas claimed there was widespread voter suppression in Trump-won states and that scores of Republican electors weren't eligible to serve. Massachusetts Representative James McGovern claimed Russians interfered with the election and challenged Alabama's electoral votes. Funny, this is the same party that had lambasted then-candidate Trump for saying he might not accept the outcome of the election if he'd lost. So, for Democrats to suggest that on January 6, 2020, we were doing something out of sorts in asking to ensure the election's integrity is wildly hypocritical. Oh, and for the record, besides 2017, Democrats also challenged the Electoral College vote certifications in 2001 and 2005.

The difference between the Republican objections in 2021 and the Democrats in 2017 is that we had legitimate concerns about election integrity backed by demonstrable facts. They just didn't like Donald Trump. Don't believe me? The reason given in the House in 2017 for why she objected to the vote certification, Representative Barbara Lee of California said, "I object because people are horrified."

For me, after having read several reports and having heard the concerns expressed by my constituents, I decided that rubber-stamping the Electoral College certification without debate would be a dereliction of my duties as a member of Congress.

There had also been several concerning questions raised about the vote count in Arizona. This is the speech I gave from the House floor objecting to Arizona's Electoral College vote certification:

"I rise to support the objection. Thank you, Madam Speaker. And to ease everyone's nerves, I want you to all know that I am not here to challenge anyone to a duel like Alexander Hamilton or Aaron Burr. Madam Speaker, my primary objection to the counting of the electoral votes of the state of Arizona is based on the Constitution and the direction of state legislatures through state law as spelled out in the following two clauses: Article 2, Section 1, Clause 2, states in part, and I quote, 'each state shall appoint in such manner as the legislature thereof may direct a number of electors and, the election clause of the Constitution provides state legislatures with explicit authority to prescribe,' and I quote, 'the times, places and manners of holding elections,' end quote. For more than three decades Arizona law, set by the state legislature, has required that voter registration end no later than 29 days before an election. This is clear. It is law. Unless amended by the state legislature, this is the way it needs to be carried out. In Arizona, the deadline for voter registration for the 2020 Presidential election was October 5, 2020. Using COVID as a reasoning, Democrats filed a lawsuit to extend this deadline by 18 days and an injunction was made by an Obama-appointed judge preventing the Arizona Secretary of State from enforcing the Constitutional deadline set by the state legislature. As a result of this frivolous, partisan lawsuit 10 extra days were added via judicial fiat to allow voter registration. These 10 days were added after voting had already begun. This is completely indefensible. You cannot change the rules of an election while it is underway and expect the American people to trust it. Now, in this 10 day period, at least 30,000 new voters registered to vote in Arizona. All of these votes are unconstitutional. It does not matter if they voted for President Trump or if they voted for Vice President Biden. They did not register in time for the election. The law states October 5th. Either we have laws, or we do not. If we allow state election laws, as set forth by state legislatures, to be ignored and manipulated on the whims of partisan lawsuits, unelected bureaucrats, unlawful procedures, and arbitrary rules, then our Constitutional Republic will cease to exist. The oath that I took this past Sunday to defend and support the Constitution makes it necessary for me to object to this travesty. Otherwise the laws passed by the legislative branch merely become suggestions to be accepted, rejected, or manipulated by those who did not pass them. Madam Speaker, I have constituents outside this building right now, I promised my voters to be their voice. In this branch of government, which I now serve, it is my separate but equal obligation to weigh in on this election and object. Are we not a government of, by and for the people? They know this election is not right and as their representative I am sent here to represent them. I will not allow the people to be ignored. Madam Speaker, it is my duty under the U.S. Constitution to object to the counting of the electoral votes of the state of Arizona. The Members who stand here today and accept the results of this concentrated, coordinated, partisan effort by Democrats where every fraudulent vote cancels out the vote of an honest American has sided with the extremist left. The United States Congress needs to make an informed decision and that starts with this objection."

The response from the Left was to call us treasonous seditionists when we were simply carrying out our duties as members of Congress—people who'd sworn to uphold the United States Constitution.

Meanwhile, lawless rioters had entered the Capitol. The Left likes to claim this was an "insurrection," which proves they don't know the meaning of the word. No one I was aware of was trying to overthrow the government, and besides, that would be awfully hard to do when no one appeared to be armed. These were people outraged at the lawlessness of the election process itself. Make no mistake, though: they may have been earnest in principle, but the actions of those who stormed the Capitol were wrong. Unequivocally. There is no justification for what they did. It was inexcusable.

Still, the delusional Left falsely claimed I helped fuel the violence. They cited one of my tweets from that day, "The Speaker has been removed from the chambers," and accused me of disclosing Speaker Nancy Pelosi's secure location. How could I possibly have done that when C-SPAN had already broadcast her departure?

By the way, the last time I checked, someone saying, "Elvis has left the building" is a call to calm an audience, not to incite violence.

The Left also pounced on another of my tweets, "Today is 1776." They claimed it was a call to revolution. Really? I saw it as a celebration of freedom. Throughout my campaign, I'd often made references to 1776 as an example of the bravery of those who stood up for freedom and to say that, if elected, I'd do the same in Congress. On January 6, I used the 1776 reference to proudly let my supporters know that, there in the House, I'd have the courage to stand up for the Constitution of the United States. It had nothing to do with violence and everything to do with freedom, not unlike President Trump's 1776 Commission, which was created to celebrate our freedom and patriotism. Desperate Democrats were trying to make a case for something that they wished had existed but, from my viewpoint, didn't.

It shouldn't be lost on anyone that these same Democrats who hypocritically throw their hands in the air when Republicans objected to certifying the Electoral College votes are the same ones trying to get rid of the Electoral College completely. They want the President to be determined by the popular vote. All the heavy hitters in the Democratic Party support the effort because, as I wrote earlier, they know it would result in heavily populated, primarily blue cities like Los Angeles, New York City, Chicago, and Boston electing the President. The Electoral College keeps that from happening and gives an equal say to people in the rest of the country as to who should be their President.

Even as I write this, there are still battles being fought to get to the bottom of the election discrepancies. Their efforts aren't about trying to prove President Trump won. They're about ensuring that future elections in the United States of America aren't run like a third-world country or a banana republic.

Free and fair elections are a cornerstone of our country and always worth fighting for.

★ ★ ★

JUST THE BEGINNING

★ ★ ★

CHAPTER 30

Keep the Faith, Keep Up the Fight

What a way to start my time in Congress, huh?!

I wish I could say things are easier now, but they're not. There's a war being fought for the soul of America, and the fight isn't between the Left and the Right or Democrat and Republican. We've gone way past that. It's a war between good and evil, between freedom and socialism. For all the progress we've made as a nation over the course of more than 200 years, in many ways, we've gone backward, primarily because of the efforts of the Left.

We live in the freest country history has ever known. The United States is such a beacon of hope around the world that a million people come here every year hoping to live the American dream. Don't believe the liberals who take a knee when the national anthem is played. If America is so oppressive, no one would willingly leave their own country to come here. Oh, and race? If America was systemically racist, it wouldn't have been able to elect Barack Obama President. Twice.

Few things have revealed the true nature of the Left as the COVID-19 pandemic. What began as "two weeks to slow the curve" became an all-out assault on the American way of life. Liberals don't even try to hide their lust for power anymore. Wannabe tyrants closed your businesses, killed your jobs, shut down your schools, ordered you to wear a mask, and, worst of all, forced you to inject yourself with a vaccine or lose your ability to freely participate in society. That choice ought to be yours, not the government's. You should be able to have a discussion with your own medical doctor and make the decision that's best for you.

Remember this: the longer you tolerate and comply with their tyranny, the worse it'll get. There's a meme that couldn't be more true that says, "At no time in history has the group of people forcing the other group of people into compliance ever been the good guys."

If you try to refute anything a leftist says, it's flagged as "misinformation" on almost every social media platform and mainstream news outlet. Don't be discouraged; misinformation is just the word they use to describe something they don't agree with. A liberal can't win an argument based on the facts because facts rarely, if ever, support their positions. If a liberal calls you a "racist" or a "Nazi," just laugh. You've won the argument because that's all they've got.

And remember, whenever a Democrat labels something "a threat to democracy," what they really mean is it's a threat to the Democrat Party.

Leftists will compare January 6 to 9/11 but look the other way when a domestic terror group like Antifa sets fire to cities like Portland, Seattle, or Minneapolis. In fact, Minneapolis's own congressional representative not only doesn't speak out against terrorism; she condones it. Ilhan Abdullahi Omar of Minnesota's 5th Congressional District has long been a terrorist sympathizer, which she's made clear repeatedly with outlandish comments and vitriolic, bigoted posts on Twitter. Among the more anti-American, pro-terrorism positions Omar's taken? Justifying the actions of ISIS terrorists by calling them the "consequence of systematic alienation." Aww, the poor things. Those misunderstood, maladjusted, and alienated guys. Well, I hate to break it to you, Ilhan, but terrorists are alienated because law-abiding Americans don't take kindly to murderous, bloodthirsty psychopaths slaughtering the innocent in the name of politics, religion, or anything else.

Omar once referred to the 9/11 hijackers/terrorists as "some people who did something," as though killing 3,000 innocent Americans is a mere day at the office. She's consistently spewed anti-American and anti-Jewish rhetoric. Yet somehow, *she's* the victim when someone jokes about her affinity for terrorism.

One day in November 2021, I shared an anecdote with some of my supporters in Colorado about running into Omar on an elevator at the Capitol. I'd made a joke that I later realized could be hurtful to people in the Islamic community, so I won't repeat it here. As a strong person of faith myself, I never want anything I say to offend someone's religion. Ever. So, I publicly apologized through all my social media channels. My statement read, "I apologize to anyone in the Muslim community I offended with my comment about Rep. Omar. I have reached out to her office to speak with her directly. There are plenty of policy differences to focus on without this unnecessary distraction." I was able to speak with Omar by phone a few days later and apologize personally. Yet, as with almost all radical leftists, she wasn't interested in mending fences. My apology wasn't good enough. Omar demanded a public apology, which, for those who are keeping score, I'd already made. It took but a second to realize there was no reasoning with this person, so I told Omar she should apologize for her anti-American, anti-Semitic, and anti-police rhetoric.

Omar hung up on me.

See, that's how the Left operates. Cancel Culture 101. There's no room for intelligent, civil discourse. When Senator Joe Manchin, a Democrat, refused to vote for Joe Biden's multi-trillion dollar social spending bill—the so-called "Build Back America" plan—because he didn't feel it was in the best interests of his constituents in West Virginia, Omar went on a vulgar tirade on MSNBC's *Velshi* show, "The excuses that he just made, I think, are complete bullshit," she told host Ali Velshi.

So, here you have a United States representative criticizing a United States senator for considering the interests of the constituents he represents. That tells you everything you need to know about the radical leftists sitting in Congress right now.

They put agenda first and Americans last.

The father of modern conservatism, an eighteenth-century statesman and philosopher named Edmund Burke, once said, "The only thing necessary for the triumph of evil is that good men should do nothing." So, be that good person who does something.

The only thing that stands between freedom and tyranny is—you.

Look at me. I was just a concerned citizen in a small town who spoke up. Before I'd ever thought about running for Congress, I went to city council meetings and spoke up. I went to a rally for a politician with policy positions I didn't care for and spoke up.

Speak up!

When twenty-one Democrats wrote a letter to Nancy Pelosi asking her to stop me from carrying my Glock pistol in DC, I spoke up. Liberals don't get to take away my Second Amendment rights. Eighty-two of my congressional colleagues stood by me, and guess what? I still carry my Glock.

That's what I call packing heat and fighting for the American way of life.

The Democrats are hell-bent and determined to destroy our country. They'll stop at nothing to destroy me and anyone working tirelessly to stop their agenda. But the fight is worth it. Socialism has never worked anywhere it's been tried. Just ask Venezuela. Someone like Sandy Cortez can tell you all day long that wealth distribution is equitable for all of us, but the only ones socialism ever works for are the elitist leaders like her. Trust me, AOC won't be giving up her Tesla.

For them, it's rules for thee, but not for me.

It's okay when a liberal like Robert De Niro says, "I'd like to punch him in the face," when talking about President Trump. And it's perfectly acceptable for then-Democratic Missouri state senator Maria Chappelle-Nadal to write on Facebook, "I hope Trump is assassinated." Imagine the outrage and consequences had a conservative written something like that about, say, Barack Obama. Chappelle-Nadal would later delete the post and escape consequences. She's not been banned by Facebook like so many conservatives have. Joe Biden himself said that if he and Donald Trump were in high school together, "I'd take him behind the gym and beat the hell out of him." Has Biden been booted from any social media platform?

We see their hypocrisy.

Take heart, though. We are the United States of America. Freedom will find a way to persevere, but it needs our help. As for me, I will always fight for the American way of life.

God bless each and every one of you, and God bless the United States of America.

ACKNOWLEDGMENTS

I would like to acknowledge my mother who brings me joy and happiness every day and always believed God had a special plan for me. To my family, for understanding it can't always be someone else standing up for our rights. To President Trump and his family for allowing a small-town girl with a gun on her hip to stand by their side in the fight for freedom. And especially to every American citizen in my district who gave me the opportunity to represent their conservative values in the United States Congress.